Soul Magic

SOUL MAGIC

First published in 2019 by Dragonfly Publications.

ISBN: 978-0-9875138-4-7

Printed by Lightning Source.
Cover Design and Layout: Ben Crompton

For information on ordering further copies of the book or to contact the author please visit nicolebayliss.com.au

10 9 8 7 6 5 4 3 2 1

A catalogue record for this book is available from the National Library of Australia

Soul Magic

Spiritual guidance and healing practices to assist with your soul's awakening.

Nicole Bayliss

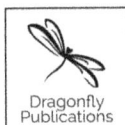

Dragonfly
Publications

This book is dedicated to my clients, who have taught me so much about life and about myself.

♡

Contents

Introduction

This book is inspired by the Monday Magic emails which I began sending out to my mailing list in 2015. Their purpose was to assist with the soul evolution that is happening for us all.

These emails were based on the soul truths that were evident all around me, both in my own life and the lives of my clients, family members and friends.

The first Monday Magic email was met with an appreciative response, and it was clear that the messages were universally needed because we are All One.

This book can be read from cover to cover or used as a guidance and healing tool by holding it in your hand, while asking a question or contemplating a challenge, and allowing a page to open.

To deepen the healing experience, I have added a meditational practice to each topic to assist you in embodying a transformational shift.

Whichever way you choose to read this book, trust it will align you to your soul and guide you towards ever greater truth, love, happiness, prosperity and light.

With love always,

Nicole x

Be still and connect with your breath.

Say the following affirmations, breathing five times between each:

I attend to myself first, before I attend to others

I choose to be kind and compassionate towards myself

I choose to forgive myself

I choose to respect myself

I choose to approve of myself

A New Year promise to self

It's wise to contemplate your intentions for the New Year, and even write a list that you can look at once in a while, but no matter what's on the list, the **most** important intention for each of us is to attend to our relationship with ourselves.

Every other relationship we have - with our partner, our children, our boss, our friends, money or work - is just a reflection of the relationship we have with ourselves.

You really are the most important person in your life.

Everyone and everything else is secondary. That doesn't mean that they're not important - they are - but you must come first.

Be still and connect with your breath.

Say the following affirmations, breathing five times
between each:

I am willing to know that I am important.

I let go of old messages that I am not important.

I am here for good reasons.

Others are important.

We are all important, and we are all One.

You are very important

♡

When you know you are important, you'll no longer seek to be validated by other people or through situations. Many of us, myself included, grew up feeling that we weren't important, because we were treated that way by our parents, school and society. It wasn't other peoples' fault because they also, deep down, felt unimportant.

Beware the wound of unimportance, which will keep re-creating relationships and situations where you feel unimportant until you address it. And beware the ego that seeks to feel important no matter what the cost. The ego hates to feel diminished.

When you are in touch with who you really are, that you are here for important reasons, you will no longer need to be shown you're important, and then life flourishes ... and then you do get validated by others, because you've validated yourself first.

Be still, connect in with the Divine Source and say the following prayer:

I surrender to You my fear of the unknown.

Please fill me with Light and cleanse me of this fear,

And take me to the place where I know

That the Universe is always supporting me in the Most Divinely right way.

Thank You.

The ego loves certainty

How boring would life be if everything was certain?
The Unknown is a very exciting place to be when you
trust and know that you're always safe because you're
supported by a loving Universe, and a very scary place if
you have no connection or faith.

The Unknown is the field of infinite possibilities! Give
up the ego's need for answers and to be certain about the
future - none of us knows for sure what tomorrow holds,
let alone beyond that, and we aren't meant to.

We simply need to live one day at a time.

"Be patient toward all that is unsolved in your heart and
try to love the questions themselves, like locked rooms
and like books that are now written in a very foreign
tongue. Do not now seek the answers, which cannot be
given you because you would not be able to live them.
And the point is, to live everything. Live the questions
now. Perhaps you will then gradually, without noticing it,
live along some distant day into the answer."
- Rainer Maria Rilke

Stay conscious of your own energy and if you feel someone or something is draining or polluting your energy field and you cannot get away, you can do the following:

Protect your energy field by pulling your aura inward (imagining your outside energy field drawn in close).

Separate your energy field from anyone who is draining or toxic by imagining two separate aura bubbles - one around you and one around them. Imagine anything said or done bouncing off your bubble.

Open your energy field when you're in harmonious situations - around high vibrational people, in nature and whenever and wherever you feel elevated - by imagining your aura expanding around you.

You are an energy field

Your energy field is sacred. Keep your vibration high by thinking loving thoughts, eating healthy foods that are right for you, drinking plenty of water, moving and connecting in regularly through silence and stillness.

Don't allow your energy field to be polluted by low vibrational people, places, situations or things. Energy always needs to find a level - and sometimes we aren't strong enough to bring the level up to ours; instead we will drop down to the vibration around us. Avoid these situations, places or people if you can, but of course sometimes we cannot avoid them.

We can use tools to manage the energy instead. Energy responds to one thing, and one thing only - consciousness!

Be still and connect with your breath. Visualise the ocean tide rolling in and rolling out.

If there is anything you have lost, see it go out on the tide. Continue to breathe as you watch the tide.

Witness the energy of the loss being returned to you on another tide. And say the following affirmation:

In Divine Law there is no loss. My abundance returns to me in Divine and perfect timing.

The tide comes in; the tide goes out

Such this the rhythm of life. Nothing stays the same and yet everything comes around full circle eventually.

We can witness the tide effect in any aspect of life. We will have periods of heightened creativity and periods of dormancy, times of deep intimacy in relationships and times of separation, periods of busy-ness and quieter times, times of gain and times of loss.

Whatever is taken away on an outgoing tide will come back again - it may be on the next tide or on a later one.

"Life is a tide; float on it. Go down with it and go up with it, but be detached. Then it is not difficult."
- **Prem Rawat**

If you're thinking about a change, about to take a risk or start something new, you can decipher whether the fear is justified or not by asking yourself the following questions:

Does the idea of this give me feelings of inspiration and joy? If so, it's a good start.

Is the result likely to lead to greater peace and happiness for me if this works out? If it's not, you may want to think again.

Is the result likely to be beneficial for those around me? If it's not, you may want to think again.

Do I feel this is likely to work out in my favour? Feel into it. There's risk and there's calculated risk.

What have I got to lose? If it doesn't work out, will you be able to handle the loss? If the possible loss feels extremely frightening and untenable, you may want to think again.

What is the worst that can happen? If the worst feels catastrophic, think again. If you know you'll recover, go ahead.

Fear

"Feel the fear and do it anyway"
- Susan Jeffers

Sometimes!

I'm sure you've heard the quote and maybe read the book of the same name. It's normal and even healthy to feel fear if you're about to make a significant change, do something new, take a risk and step out of your comfort zone.

Most fear is based on a fear of loss or failure. Fear is our mind trying to protect us - sometimes it's helpful and sometimes it's not. The fearful mind doesn't know the difference between constructive change and destructive change.

Be still and connect with your breath.

Say the following affirmations three times, breathing five times between each:

It is safe to follow my truth

I am here to follow my truth

I release all fear of judgment and criticism

My truth is my way.

Follow your Truth

ॐ

What is your truth? It's the path that feels right for you.

It may not seem right to others. That's because your truth may not be their truth. We are all here to express ourselves and to be who we want to be. The **me** I am meant to express may be quite different to the **you which** you wish to express.

Be aware that when you decide to be true to yourself and do what you truly want to do and say what you truly want to say, you may be met by hostile reactions and criticism. This is a normal part of transformation.

"If the majority doesn't laugh at you, beware that you must be saying something wrong. When the majority thinks you are a fool, only then is there some possibility of you being a wise man".
-Lao Tzu

Be still, connect in with the Divine Source and say the following prayer:

I surrender all my worries and feelings of overwhelm to You

Thank You for reminding me that all I need to deal with is today

And that by doing what I need to do today

I create my Divinely right future.

Overwhelm

It is difficult to make progress when you're feeling overwhelmed. Life has a way of throwing circumstances at us that can feel overwhelming. Our own minds have a way of throwing thoughts at us that can feel overwhelming too. The mind brings the past into the Now and the future into the Now, yet the reality is that all we ever have to handle is this one present moment.

We get led astray by the ego mind that convinces us we need to **fix this** and we need to be **over there** in the fixed place in order to be happy. But this is simply not true!

We can still be dealing with a challenge and be happy! How? By embracing whatever is in the present moment and dealing with it in the way that feels Divinely right for us in that present moment. Trying to **fix the future** is pointless. That is what puts us into overwhelm. By dealing with this one present moment in the Divinely right way, we make a positive impact on the future.

All you have is now. Allow the future to take care of itself.

Be still and connect with your breath.

Say the following affirmations three times, breathing
five times between each:

I release all fear of expressing myself

It is safe to express myself

It is safe to speak my truth

I speak my truth with love.

You are here to express yourself

Even if you feel that you are but a drop of water in an ocean, your job is to express yourself. You are an important part of the Universal Whole. You have a purpose.

Express everything - not just your **positive thoughts** that come out as positive words, but everything that is your truth. Sometimes what must be expressed is your frustration, your pain and your fears. They are all just as much a part of you as the loving thoughts and feelings.`

Expressing yourself and your truth is an act of love towards yourself, and therefore an act of love towards others. What goes unexpressed doesn't disappear. It sits in your energy field. and if it's fearful, it will create havoc in your life.

By expressing all of your truth - the good, the bad and the ugly - energy gets moving and results in healing.

Be still, connect in with the Divine Source and say the following prayer:

I surrender to You my desire to follow my bliss

And I surrender to You the burdens in my life

I am willing to accept that both my bliss and life's burdens are important

Please guide me to do what is Divinely right and good and true

So that I may live my full potential

Thank You.

Bliss and burden

Life isn't always blissful. Many of us are burdened with responsibilities not of our own conscious making, and obligations that seem unavoidable.

That's because life contains everything. If we were to follow our bliss with complete disregard for anyone or anything else, the stakes are high that we will end up alone, unloved and unliked.

Life is a balancing act. At times, it's Divinely right to follow your bliss and do exactly what **you** want to do, and at other times it's Divinely right to think about the **big picture** and to attend to others' needs simply because you know it's the right thing to do, and that by doing so, you feel at peace.

Life will present you with circumstances where you need to choose one or the other. Choose wisely! There is no right or wrong choice; simply that which serves you and that which does not.

If you are feeling resistance in any area of your life, here is a question to ask yourself:

What do I have to believe for this to be painful?

And whatever that belief is, know it isn't true.

Be still and say the following prayer:

I surrender all resistance to You.

Thank you for bringing me to a place of acceptance

That everything is in my life for a reason

Thank You for revealing to me why that is.

Illusion

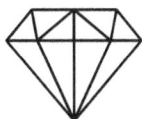

The world is an illusion because it exists as you interpret it.

It's not what happens to you; it's what you **think** about what happens to you that is the problem. Nothing, in truth, is a problem; it is just What Is.

It becomes a problem because we overlay it with our judgments, our desires, our beliefs and our expectations that are in opposition to the What Is.`

The What Is is the Divine Hand at work. If it hurts, why does it hurt? If it makes you angry, why?

The ego mind wants life to go its way - it cannot see or know that the very thing you didn't want to happen is happening for your highest good and will ultimately lead to something good if you accept it and are willing to see the good in it.

Be still and connect with your breath.

Say the following affirmation five times, breathing five times between each:

Feel yourself right here, right now in this present moment.

As you breathe in and out, allow yourself to deepen into this present moment.

Feel the presence of the invisible Universal energy run through you.

Feel it around you.

Listen to the outside sounds and feel the Divine presence in all that you hear.

Connection

When you connect to **What Is** right here and right now,
you connect to the Divine.

To be connected, fully embrace what is right here, right
now, with all of your senses. When meditating, embrace
everything you can hear, feel, taste. smell and even see. A
friend, a musician, was practising her flute on the beach
when a woman approached her and said "Do you mind?
I'm trying to meditate! Please play your flute elsewhere."

Meditation isn't about shutting the world out; it's about
allowing the world in. It's not demanding that the world
be quiet; it's about becoming quiet enough within to
really feel the moment, whatever that moment looks and
feels like. In that moment, we feel the Divine at work and
know that it is all perfect.

Life can be lived on the surface; or it can be experienced
more deeply. To connect more deeply with everyone and
everything in your daily life, open your senses. When out
walking, don't just look at a tree; become the tree. When
relating to another person, don't just attempt to listen to
the person; become the person, because we are all One.

Be still, connect in with the Divine Source and say the following prayer:

I surrender this situation to You

I am open to signs and guidance as to what to do next

If I am meant to keeping moving ahead with this, thank You for showing me

And if I am meant to let this go now, thank You for showing me.

The Inevitable

Try as we may, we cannot stave off the inevitable.

*There are certain things in life that are inevitable - one we all share is death - but apart from death, there will be other **inevitables** that we cannot stop from happening.*

This is because we all have soul contracts that we've signed up for, and there's no getting out of them.

Have you ever attempted to stop something from happening but try as you may, it still happened? That's because it was meant to happen. Or perhaps you wanted for something to happen, but try as you may, it just wouldn't happen. That's because it wasn't meant to happen.

Trying to make something happen or make something not happen can be like trying to hold back the tide. It's pointless and a waste of energy. This is not to say that you weren't meant to try, but at some point you've got to realise when it's time to let go, surrender and allow whatever is meant to take place to take place!

Everything, even those things you don't want to happen, is leading to your highest good.

If you're feeling anxious about the future, take a deep breath in and out and feel yourself present in the here and now.

Remind yourself that all that matters is this present moment, because right now that is all there is!

Then ask yourself what is it I'm fearing about the future?

When you get your answer, ask yourself Is there anything I can do about that now?

If there is something constructive that you can do now, then do it, but if there isn't, relax! And say the following affirmation:

I live in the now, and I allow the future to take care of itself.

Fear of the future

Fear of the future creates anxiety.

It comes from the ego mind which cannot tolerate the unknown, but the unknown is the field of all possibilities. There is no growth in the known!

The future is always a place of light; not darkness. There is so much you don't know and you cannot know. As I look back on my life, I laugh with joy.

During my Dark Night of the Soul, there is no way I could have known how my life would turn out, and that I would be a healer and that I could live such joy from day to day.

Life is simply one present moment after the other, wanting to be lived.

Be still and connect with your breath. Feel into your body from top to toe.

Notice any sensations and feelings in your body.

Connect in with your third eye chakra just between your eyebrows, visualising a deep indigo blue.

This is your centre of knowing. Continue to breathe while focusing on this chakra.

Now visualise white healing light streaming through your third eye chakra, releasing all blocks to your truth.

Clarity

True clarity will never come from the thinking reasoning mind.

The reasoning mind will have you going around in circles, writing pros and cons lists, trying to work out the best way forward, but rarely will you feel fully aligned with what the mind comes up with, because you are a multi-dimensional being and the reasoning mind is not.

When you ask the Supreme Intelligence for guidance and lay aside the reasoning mind, you are tapping the Universal supply of all knowledge; and anything you need to know will be revealed to you.

The problem for many people, however, is that their minds are so busy they aren't able to be receptive to what is being shown to them! Learning to be quiet and still is the key to gaining true clarity.

To live intuitively is to live fourth-dimensionally. Following an intuitive hunch, you escape all complications and friction

Be still and connect with your breath. As you feel your sadness or sorrow, notice where you feel it in your body.

Feel its physical sensations.

Do not try to push it away.

Lovingly acknowledge it.

Does it have a shape? A texture? A colour? Does it move or is it still?

Does it have a message for you?

Don't be concerned if there is no message. Everything must be lovingly acknowledged.

Sorrow

Whenever sorrow comes, be kind to it. For God has placed a pearl in sorrow's hand
- Rumi

Sorrow is a part of life. It always has been and always will be. Whatever you feel sad about, accept the sadness. Feel the sadness. Every emotion must be accepted and felt if we are to process life and enjoy life.

Don't judge your sadness. Allow it to be there. It is what it is. Don't judge yourself for feeling sad by buying into the illusion that we are supposed to be constantly happy.

How can we know happiness if we haven't experienced sadness? How can we appreciate the light without having known the dark?

If you are in resistance to anything in your life right now, or are fearful about anything, take a deep breath in and out and say:

I accept this just as it is and I choose to see this through eyes of love.

Say the following prayer:

I surrender this situation to You.

Thank You for helping me to see this through eyes of love.

Perception

Change your perception of things and you will change your reality ...

How you perceive things will either empower you or disempower you. How you perceive something to be is not necessarily reality. Our ego mind loves putting a fearful spin on things. It will look at circumstances through the filter of fear. Circumstances look very different when looked through the filter of love.

We lose a lot of energy when we look through fearful eyes. When we look at life through loving eyes, we accept it and can then put our energy towards resolving the situation. We work with the Universe, instead of against it.

Nothing happens by accident. Perceive everything through loving eyes and accept it all.

Be still, connect in with the Divine Source and say the following prayer:

I surrender my pain to You

Please help me to accept this transformational process

Take me to the place where all is peace and love.

Darkness and dawn

The darkest part of the night always precedes the dawn.

Things can sometimes get worse before they get better, even if we have surrendered a situation to the Universe for resolution. If we can see this as a necessary part of a healing process, it makes the journey a little easier.

If you are going through difficulties, know that they are in your life for your spiritual growth.

Do not resent your challenges because you will work against them; accept them and work with them, and if things get worse, remind yourself that the darkest part of the night always precedes the dawn.

True transformation isn't painless ... it involves pain. "Despair is the necessary prerequisite before we go to the next level of consciousness."
- Ram Dass

Contemplate where you are struggling.

Be still, connect in with the Divine Source and say the following prayer:

I surrender this situation to You.

Thank You for the perfect resolution in Divine and perfect timing.

Surrender, trust, be patient and miracles will happen.

Surrender

Surrender, surrender, surrender!

Surrendering is a far more powerful thing to do than striving, pushing, controlling or forcing.

To surrender doesn't mean to **give up**. It means to let go and trust that there is always a higher intelligence that is ultimately in charge.

So we let go and we give the Supreme Intelligence permission to orchestrate, permission to work out the **how**, for it knows far better than we do how to go about things.

Thy will be done.

Be still and connect with your breath.

Say the following affirmations three times, breathing five times between each:

The Divine Blueprint of me already exists.

My true potential is here within my cells

I now release all blocks to living my true potential

I allow myself to expand in all areas of my life.

Intuitive path

The intuitive path is the path to your highest good. You are unique and all the answers you need already exist within you.

The most Divine, happy, successful version of you already exists within you too.

There is nothing you need to **do** or to **add** to you. You simply need to sit with yourself and be still and you will begin to let go of the illusions that trap you and keep you stuck in fear.

True transformation is a series of **letting go, peeling the onion** layer by layer until we arrive at our truth, our True Self.

Be still and connect with your breathe and sit with the following questions:

What do I need to let go of in my home?

What do I need to let go of in my diary?

What do I need to let go of in my mind?

Continue to breathe and feel the spaciousness of this present moment.

Follow through with clearing out all that is no longer needed.

Simplicity

"In character, in manner, in style, in all things ... the supreme excellence is simplicity"
- **Henry Wordsworth Longfellow**

In this age of information overload, sophistication and complexity, we can forget the power of simplicity. Simplicity brings spaciousness and clarity of mind.

We all have the ability to create more simplicity in our lives. Declutter your home, let go of things that keep you unnecessarily busy with little reward, be mindful of what you put in your diary, resist gossip and other people's dramas.

Be still and connect with your breath.

Say the following affirmations three times, breathing five times between each:

I give thanks for the time I have

I love the time I have

There is always enough time

I have the perfect amount of time to do what I am here to do.

Time and timing

"The butterfly counts not months but moments, and still has time enough"
- Rabindranath Tagore

One of the greatest barriers to happiness and inner peace is an unloving relationship with time.

If we believe we don't have enough time, we won't have it. If we believe that time is something we must fight against, we will find ourselves constantly fighting time. If we believe that time is running out, it will run out!

Our True Self sees time as a gift and as a friend. And our True Self knows the truth about time:

We always have enough time to do what is in our highest good to do. When we use our time lovingly, we will be given more time (and unlovingly, less time). Time doesn't run out for anything that is part of the Divine plan for our lives.

Practise gratitude for the time you have and it will expand. Believe and feel that there is a lack of time, and time will contract.

Be still and connect with your breath.

Say the following affirmation five times, breathing five
times between each:

I am willing to become aware of myself, my thoughts and
my actions

I am willing to understand myself.

Awareness

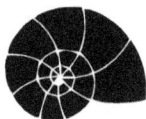

You can only change what you understand, and the only way to understand yourself is through self-awareness.

Awareness is learning to watch and observe yourself in every situation. When you got angry with someone, were you aware or were you identifying with and locked into the anger? Later, when you had calmed down and had the time, did you study your experience and attempt to understand it? Where did it come from? What brought it on?

There is no other way to self-awareness except through self-observation and examination.

What you do not understand about yourself you will not be aware of. It will be repressed, so you don't change. But when you can observe yourself, you will begin to understand yourself, and so you can change for the better.

To be self-aware, be willing to wake up from being on **auto-pilot**. For most of us, self-awareness takes time and happens gradually, but this process of transformation brings with it the reward of happiness.

Be still and connect with your breath, and visualise your desire.

Feel like you already have it.

Connect in with the Divine Source and say the following prayer:

I surrender this to You

If it is in my highest good, thank you for making it happen and if it is not, thank You for sending me what is ultimately for my highest good.

Wanting

There is nothing wrong with desiring certain things. It's human nature. But beware the ego mind, which can have you convinced that a certain thing will make you happy. How many times have you manifested something you really wanted only to find it didn't fulfill you or you realised that it also had negative aspects?

Everything that you want will have both positive and negative aspects to it, so it's wise to become aware of them before drawing your vision to you. If you want something, by all means, visualise it, ask for it but also **surrender**. The act of surrender means you surrender your desire to the Universe by detaching from it.

The Universe knows far better than you do what will fulfill you. It has much greater plans for you than you do for yourself!

Wanting isn't the correct vibration from which to manifest; it only creates one thing and that is more wanting!

Be still and connect with your breath. Contemplate what you truly desire.

Sense any need to hurry, to push or force things to happen sooner than is possible or comfortable.

Say the following affirmations three times, breathing five times between each:

I now release the need to hurry, force or push

Everything has its own Divine timing

I allow this to manifest in Divine and perfect timing.

Shortcuts

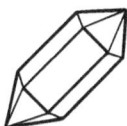

"There are no shortcuts to any place worth going"
- **Beverly Sills**

It's our ego's nature to want to hurry things up, to seek the quick fix and to want to know just how long something is going to take and when we're going to get there. The ego isn't patient.

Too often we choose the band-aid approach or the quick--fix because we don't want to **waste time** or take the time to achieve something that is worthwhile.

If you truly want to do something, but are choosing not to because it's going to take too long, remember that time is going to pass anyway, so you may as well do the thing you really want to do, and take the time to do it properly.

Roses that are forced to open in a hot house rarely have a scent and die faster than those grown in a garden.

Be still and connect with your breath. Breathe in and out of your heart, your centre of love and forgiveness.

With every breath in, breathe in love, and every breath out, let go of the need to judge.

Do this for ten breaths. Say the following affirmation:

I lovingly allow _____ to be as they are and I acknowledge that they are doing the best they can.

Judging

ॐ

Character defects are not where we are **bad** but where we are wounded, and we've all been wounded; we're all flawed. By focussing on someone else's faults and seeing them as guilty, we block love from flowing.

Those who we don't like and judge are a reflection of something we have repressed and don't like and judge in ourselves

Acceptance creates miracles. When others feel accepted just the way they are, often they change for the better - not always, but often.

Give up judgment and you will begin to feel better in yourself. Kindness and compassion are good for your mind, your body and your spirit.

Be still and connect with your breath. Ask yourself:

In what ways am I not being true to myself?

Why?

What is the fear?

Acknowledge the fear or fears that come up. Lovingly accept the fear.

Whatever we accept will change; what we resist persists.

True to self

"To thine own self be true, and as night follows day, thoust cannot be untrue to any man"
- William Shakespeare

Being true to yourself takes courage, because being true to yourself can mean upsetting other people, letting go of situations and things that are no longer good for you, and not being liked in the process. Being true to yourself can bring up your three greatest fears:

Fear of rejection
Fear of loss
Fear of not being liked or loved.

It is perfectly understandable that we have these fears. They are held deep within our psyche. Fear of rejection and not being loved begins when we are born. If we are rejected and not loved, we won't survive. And fear of loss in any way will also threaten our sense of survival.

Yet, if we acknowledge them, we bring them out of the darkness and into the light. In the light, fear loses its power.

Be still, connect in with the Divine Source and say the following prayer:

I surrender my indecision to You.

Thank You for guiding my mind towards the Divinely right choice.

Thank You for casting from my mind all that does not serve me.

Decisions

Decisions, decisions.

Facing a major decision can be terrifying, because we're fearful of making the **wrong** decision; fearful of what we may lose at the cost of what we might gain. It's so much easier when life makes the decision for us, but sometimes we're faced with making that difficult decision.

The old saying **when in doubt, don't** is a wise one. If you don't have clarity, how can you make a decision? Sometimes, if you just wait, life will show you what the best choice is.

If however, you need to make a decision quickly, don't choose out of fear, because that won't serve you in the long run. Choose out of love. What will give you a feeling of expansion and inspiration? It may take you out of your comfort zone, but growth will always serve you.

People rarely regret the things they did; they regret the things they didn't do.

Look at yourself in the mirror and say:

I am willing to love and accept you.

If you find it difficult to love and accept yourself, do this practice daily until you are able to say I love and accept you.

Authentic vs Perfect

Are you choosing to be authentic or striving to be perfect?

Choosing to be authentic requires self-acceptance - acceptance of our positive qualities as well as our faults.

When you fully accept yourself, you love yourself and that love will shine through as the Authentic You. Authenticity attracts people who accept you and love you because you're accepting and loving yourself!

Striving to be perfect comes from the ego, the false self, that wants to present a front to the world because the ego won't accept our own human faultiness.

Accept yourself and the world will accept you too.

Be still and connect with your breath.

Notice your thoughts come and go, and as you do this, know that they are just thoughts. They have no power over you.

Your True Self is in charge. Your True Self can recognise the ego mind's destructive thoughts.

Say the following affirmation five times, breathing five times between each:

My energy flows towards my highest good always.

Energy direction

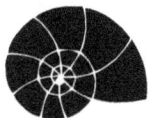

Where are you directing your energy?

Your energy comes through your thoughts, your words and your actions. Whatever you put your energy into will expand and grow, and whatever you take it away from will wither and die.

Become aware of where your energy goes. If you put your energy into doing the things you love and into relationships with people who inspire you, support you and care about you, and into activities that are nurturing to your mind, body and spirit, your life will expand in wondrous ways.

Conversely, if you put your energy into doing things that you're not passionate about but feel you **should** do, into relationships with people who drain you, confuse you or put you down, and into activities that are destructive to your mind, body or spirit, your life will contract in a tragic way.

Be still and connect with your breath. Relax.

Imagine yourself floating in a stream.

This is the Universal Flow. Accepting the What Is and working with it and not against it.

With every breath out, relax and let go.

Say the following affirmation five times, breathing five times between each:

I relax and let go and allow my dreams to manifest in Divine and perfect timing.

Swimming upstream

There may be times in our lives where we need to swim upstream, like salmon struggling against the odds to return to their birthplace and spawn their young.

You know you're swimming upstream when you're putting out tremendous effort in some aspect of your life. This is well and good if you are achieving results, but none of us can continue swimming upstream indefinitely. At the end of their journey, salmon die. They are completely worn out by their efforts.

Life can be so much simpler and easier than we make it. By taking a **downstream** approach, we can create our dreams in a more relaxed and joyful way. We will reach our goals when they are ready to manifest.

There will be both upstream times and downstream times in life. Become aware when you're swimming upstream - forcing, pushing, battling - and ask yourself if this is truly necessary (sometimes it is), Whenever you can, opt for the downstream - it is so much more enjoyable!

Be still and connect with your breath.

Feel into your heart chakra at the centre of your chest, your centre of love.

Picture a green spinning vortex of energy.

Connect to the love that already exists within you.

Say the following affirmations three times, breathing five times between each:

I am a being of infinite love.

I let go of all that isn't love.

I relate to everyone and everything with love.

Love

♡

"One word frees us, and that word is love"
- **Sophocles**

Whatever you do, do it with love. Any task undertaken without love will not create the optimum outcome.

With whomever you are communicating - a loved one, a colleague, a client, a difficult person - communicate with love.

Whatever you are worried or concerned about, think about it with love.

Love is the transformer. It is the healer. It is really that simple.

Every problem was either created or fuelled by a lack of love.

Love is your natural state, and all that isn't love isn't real.

Be still and connect with your breath.

Feel your own presence.

Ask yourself the follow questions:

Where in my life do I need to make the space to listen more?

Where in my life do I need to let go of fixing or rescuing?

Listening

"Courage is what it takes to stand up and speak; courage
is also what it takes to sit down and listen"
- **Winston Churchill**

So many of us want to be heard, but do we really listen?
Learning to actively listen to someone and appreciate
their position even when we don't agree is an act of
healing - both for you and the other.

Being willing to listen to another person is an act of
generosity, giving time and space for them to express
themselves without interruption.

When you're listening, learn to hear what isn't being
said, as well as what is. This will be shown to you through
body language.

Attempting to fix or rescue disempowers the other
person, while actively listening with loving presence will
empower and heal.

Be still and connect with your breath.

Say the following affirmations three times, breathing
five times between each:

I courageously face my challenges

I choose actions that create good karma

I make choices that enhance my self-esteem.

Never do these three things

Never do any of these three things if you want to live a fulfilling and conscious life.

Never use fear as a justification for avoiding life. It is better to face a fearful situation than ignore it.

Never do things you will have to karmically punish yourself for. What goes around comes around eventually. We don't get away with anything!

Never do anything that causes you to lose self-esteem. How you feel about yourself affects every aspect of your life.

Be still and connect with your breath. Feel yourself present. Contemplate any addictions you may have.

Connect to your heart and send yourself love and compassion.

If there is anyone in your life who is struggling with addiction, send them love and compassion.

Say the following affirmation five times, breathing five times between each:

I am willing to become conscious and to seek wholeness in ways that serve me.

Searching for wholeness

We are all searching for wholeness, be it consciously or unconsciously.

If we are searching consciously, we will choose activities to enhance our growth and evolution such as spending time in nature, eating healthy food, exercising and seeking spiritual connection.

If we're not searching for wholeness consciously, we are still searching for it. The unconscious search for wholeness will usually take us down the path of addiction - addiction to alcohol, drugs, sugar, cigarettes, shopping, gambling, porn and other people.

When viewed through this lens, we can have compassion for ourselves or others who are in the grip of addiction, because at the heart of any addiction is a search for healing.

The power is within all of us to wake up and seek wholeness consciously.

Be still and connect with your breath. Notice your breath, the rise and fall of your chest and the sensations in your nostrils as you breathe.

Allow yourself to be totally present in this moment. Observe yourself sitting here meditating.

Continue to sit and notice your thoughts coming and going.

This part of you that can observe has the power to examine as well. If you have any disturbing thoughts, ask yourself the following question:

Is this absolutely true?

Say the following affirmation five times, breathing five times between each:

I let go of assumptions and I am willing to know the truth.

Assumptions

How often are you making assumptions that may not necessarily be true?

The ego mind is very good at making assumptions.

Assumptions are uninvestigated thinking, which can lead us into unnecessary pain and negative outcomes, because we create from these assumptive thoughts.

Assumptions can be wishful thinking or they can be fearful or negative thinking. Either way, they aren't necessarily aligned with reality.

Notice how often you can jump to conclusions. Begin to investigate your thinking.

Ask yourself **How true is this thought?** *It may be the truth, or it may not be, or it may be partially true. Just by examining the thought, it will lose its power.*

Be still and connect with your breath.

Feel the earth beneath you and send her love.

Connect with your heart and the consciousness and wisdom that is there.

Allow it to radiate from you out into the world.

Visualise the world as you would like it to be.

Give thanks to Divine Intelligence for this manifestation.

The World

At times we may feel profound sadness for what is
happening in the world.

We can do our bit by living congruent to our values, but
on a physical level, most of it is out of our control.

On the spiritual level however, we have far more power.

Put forth your intentions for the world as a whole.

Take time to meditate and visualise an ideal world - a
peaceful world, a kind world, a world full of light.

Give thanks to Divine Intelligence for its manifestation.

When out in nature, feel the earth beneath your feet and
send it love and gratitude for all the earth provides.

Be still and connect with your breath. Feel yourself in this present moment.

Picture the timeline of your life before you. You are standing in the now.

Face your past and visualise washing away all your regrets with white light.

And now visualise white light washing through you now, clearing you of the energy of regret.

Turn now and see the path leading to your future.

Wash the path down with white light, ensuring that your future is free of regrets.

Regret

Regret - a feeling of sorrow or disappointment about something that has happened or been done.

Regret serves only one purpose - to learn a lesson from the past which you can take with you into the future.

Other than that, regret is not helpful.

Dwelling on choices you have made in the past and wishing you could change that choice is pointless.

You did what you thought was right at the time, and therefore it was right. Dwelling on things that happened which you had no control over is also pointless. Forgive and move on.

There is no way to change the past. Wishing it was different only drains your energy and robs you of the opportunities in the present moment. Love the past - all of it - for every part of it served you in some way.

Be still and connect with your breath.

If you are feeling anxious or fearful, notice the sensations and where you physically feel them.

Ask yourself the following question:

What am I in fear of?

Say the following affirmations three times, breathing five times between each:

I acknowledge my fear of _____

I surrender this fear.

Nothing that is truly important can ever be taken away from me.

Fear

F alse
E vidence
A ppearing
R eal

Fear is your only adversary - fear of loss, fear of rejection, fear of failure, fear of criticism ... the list is endless.

Fear draws to you the very thing that you don't want. Fear loss? There will be loss. Fear rejection? There will be rejection.

We cannot get rid of fear, but by facing it, it loses its power. We see it for what it is - the ego mind that thinks in terms of catastrophe.

The True You knows that nothing of any true importance or value can ever be taken away from you.

Fear underlies every anxiety. We cannot conquer fear until we are faced with every aspect of our fear. Welcome fear! Be willing to shine a light on it. Observe it. Feel it.

Fear inverted becomes Faith.

Be still and connect with your breath.

Contemplate all that you have to be grateful for in the here and now, no matter how small.

Take a few minutes and let the list grow.

Say the following affirmations three times, breathing five times between each:

I am so appreciative for what I already have. Thank You.

Now take a few minutes to visualise the future you desire. As you imagine it, feel the feelings as if you already have it.

Say the following affirmations three times, breathing five times between each:

I am so appreciative of my ideal future. Thank You.

The bridge of gratitude

You're here but you want to be there.

The more you want to be **there**, the more you don't want to be **here**. You may despise what's here and now, thinking you'll be happy when you get that job, find **the one**, make that money or resolve a particular problem. The ego mind is up to its tricks again!

The bridge between where you are now and having what you want in the future is gratitude. Be grateful for all that you have now. **Feel** gratitude now. When you really value and appreciate what you have now, you will create the perfect vibration that creates what you want in the future. Don't let your ego mind take you into the vibration of lack, from which nothing can be manifested.

Practise gratitude on a daily basis. Start a list of all you are grateful for and grow it each day. And take it one step further - be grateful for all your challenges for without them you wouldn't grow and evolve.

Notice how you begin to feel full and not empty, peaceful and not conflicted, rich and not poor.

Be still and connect with your breath.

Breathe in and out of your heart and send yourself love and compassion.

Feel appreciation towards yourself and how far you have come.

Say the following affirmations three times, breathing five times between each:

Healing is a process and I embrace the journey.

I accept that challenges will appear on my healing journey.

I stay determined, for patience obtains all things.

Changing a pattern

An interesting thing happens when we begin to change a pattern. A situation may appear to become worse for a while. This is a sign that the situation is beginning to move. For example:

You're working on becoming healthy and you get sick

You're working on your low self-esteem and you're treated poorly.

You're working on being a more loving person and you have a fight with your partner.

You're working on increasing your prosperity and you lose your wallet.

Don't give up! Old patterns get magnified to present to you a healing opportunity. Anything that brings up fear and fearful thinking must be faced, so as to neutralise it with loving thought. These things will keep being presented to you until the pattern is cleared.

Stay determined, don't give up. Patience obtains all things.

Be still and connect with your breath. Know that right here, right now in this present moment you are free!

Feel and sense the spaciousness within you.

Feel the spaciousness all around you.

Say the following affirmations three times, breathing five times between each:

I am willing to know that I am free.

I have the freedom to choose new thoughts.

I have the freedom to choose new behaviours.

I open up to the many choices available to me.

I am free!

Freedom

You are the only jailer that ever surfaces in your own life.

The only thing that is getting in the way of your freedom is your mind. You have the freedom to choose new thoughts, new perceptions and ideas and new ways of being. Even prisoners have the freedom to choose these things.

There is only ever the fearful thought or the loving thought. Fearful thoughts will keep you imprisoned; loving thoughts will set you free.

The next time you begin a sentence with the words **I have to... STOP!** Allow your mind to open up to the alternatives. And even if it is in your highest good to do the thing you feel trapped by, choose to do it with a loving mindset.

Wherever you have choice, take it. You always have the power to choose at some level, no matter what your circumstances. You have a myriad of choices available to you. Your mind is your only jailer.

Whenever you realise that you have the power to be free, freedom follows.

Be still and connect with your breath.

Choose that you will sit with yourself today with unconditional love.

When your mind wanders or you experience emotions, lovingly observe your thoughts and feelings.

Focus back on the breath whenever you gain awareness that your mind has wandered off.

If any thoughts or feelings are uncomfortable, face your *enemy* with loving presence.

Do this for twenty minutes.

The enemy within

No enemy can exist **out there** when there are no enemies within.

Let go of seeking happiness outside of yourself. Nothing will bring you happiness for long, for everything in this world is impermanent.

To find true happiness, we must get to know ourselves - by turning inwards and not outwards, being willing to examine ourselves and our reactions.

This way you will begin to understand yourself.

All our enemies exist within us. This is why the Buddhists tell us that to meditate, to sit with oneself, is **true fearlessness**.

Be still and connect with your breath.

Say the following affirmation five times, breathing five times between each:

I am willing to become aware of the patterns that do not serve me.

Blind Spots

"When patterns are broken, new worlds emerge"
- Tuli Kupferberg

We all have our blind spots - self-made patterns that we may not be aware of. Some of our patterns will serve us; others won't. Negative patterns may exist within us because we are unaware they're even there. The ego mind will blind us, convincing us that we're a victim of the world **out there**, when in fact there's a pattern in us that creates the negativity.

It takes presence and awareness to become aware of our negative life patterns, and sometimes even this won't be enough. This is where an objective view can be helpful - from a counsellor, coach or healer.

Some people shy away from seeing a healing professional because it feels like an admission that there is something wrong with them. But we are all have blind spots - counsellors, coaches and healers see other counsellors, coaches and healers because they can't see their blind spots either!

When you seek outside help, you are taking affirmative action to become aware of and transcend the negative patterns that are creating what you don't want.

Be still and connect with your breath.

Say the following affirmation five times, breathing five times between each:

I am willing to expand my awareness.

Awareness

Awareness is a state of being that is pure presence ...

When we are fully present, whatever we choose to do will
be Divinely right, because we are not bringing the past
into the now, nor drawing the future into the now.

In the present moment we break through the cage of our
conditioning and follow the truth that exists right here
and right now.

Whatever arises out of awareness in the present
moment, without any effort or practice, will be perfect.

When you make awareness your highest intention,
everything else will fall into place!

Be still and connect with your breath.

Contemplate your current challenges and acknowledge any feelings of hopelessness, negativity or pessimism.

Connect in with the Divine Source and say the following prayer:

I surrender my challenges to You.

I surrender to you any sense of hopelessness, negativity and pessimism.

Please fill me with Your light.

Please give me patience, positivity and optimism

That all will be resolved in Divine and perfect timing.

Thank You.

Time heals all things

Nature has a way of reminding us that nothing stays the same and that there are always new beginnings.

When we are in the midst of challenges, it's hard to believe that things can get better, but better they do get if we are patient and optimistic, as expressed in these words by Patience Strong:

If you do not try to force the pace of providence,

Time will work things out and with a happy consequence.

Difficult your life may be and hard your present plight.

But wait before you grumble. Give time to put it right.

Be still and connect with your breath.

Imagine inside of you is your younger self - a little girl or boy who wants to play and have fun.

Imagine that he or she is sitting on your lap.

Ask your inner child what he or she needs right now.

Allow yourself to listen for the answer.

It may come in the form or your inner child answering you, or as a feeling or an idea. Then commit to doing it.

Say the following affirmation five times, breathing five times between each:

My inner child is a being of love, light and joy. I honour and love my inner child

Make time for your inner child

"*To enter the Kingdom of Heaven you must be as little children*"
- Jesus

This is a poignant reminder from Jesus that in our grown-up world of obligations, demands and expectations, we need to make time for our inner child.

Your inner child is the part of you that is playful, innocent and uncomplicated. Your inner child is naturally creative and enjoys freedom and fun. He or she is a very real part of you, and if you overlook your inner child for too long, life becomes dull and dreary.

Make time for your inner child by going within and asking your inner child **How do you feel?** and **What would you like to do?**.

Then take your inner child on an outing doing something playful and fun - go dancing, play on the swings at the park, build a sandcastle on the beach, do a painting or eat an ice cream - anything that makes your heart sing and doesn't involve responsibility or work.

Be still and connect with your breath.

Feel into your heart which is the window to your soul.

Ask yourself the following question:

What do I love?

Allow the answers to come.

There are no right or wrong answers.

Let your soul speak to you. You may want to write the answers down.

List at least fifty things.

Soul alignment

🕉

If we want to be truly happy, we must pay attention to our soul's messages.

The soul wants to feel love, joy, inspiration and freedom. That's what we're here to learn and to be.

We all have obligations and tasks that are necessary, but we need to balance these with the things that feed our soul.

What those things are will be unique to you.

The more you listen to your soul and follow its desires, the more opportunities for soul freedom will be given to you.

Be still and connect with your breath.

Say the following affirmation five times, breathing five times between each:

I am willing to let go of illusions and to know who I really am.

Disillusionment

"Disillusionment with yourself must precede
enlightenment"
- **Vernon Howard**

Disillusionment, and all the mixed emotions that go with
it, is a normal part of growth and transformation.

We must constantly let go of old ideas and impressions
of who we think we are, so as to discover a renewed and
more enlightened version of ourselves.

Life is a series of releasing the veils of illusion that keep
us trapped.

If you are going through disillusionment in any area of
your life, lovingly accept it. It is bringing you closer to
who you really are.

Be still and connect with your breath.

Say the following affirmations three times, breathing five times between each:

I am already perfect, whole and complete

I am a Divine being who is connected to the Divine Intelligence

Everything I need is already within me

The essence of me is love.

You are not a victim!

"Our human relationships change fundamentally once we stop looking for fulfilment or our sense of self in others"
- Eckhart Tolle

You are not a victim! We must stop allowing other people and circumstances to define who we are.

Our ego is the victim. It is an accumulation of woundedness and unexamined beliefs.

This is the truth of who you really are ;

You are already perfect, whole and complete.

You are a Divine being who has access to the Divine Intelligence

Everything you need is already within you.

The essence of you is love.

None of this can ever be taken away from you.

Be still and connect with your breath.

Contemplate how often you focus on the unwanted things in your life.

Imagine that there is a cord between you and all the unwanted situations and things.

See it being cut and all those undesirables detaching from you, and floating off into the light.

And now allow yourself to envision all that you want until you are smiling.

Thank the Universe in advance for this manifestation.

Intention

We have enough people who tell it like it is - we now need to tell it like it can be.

While you may be living your current reality, you have the power to change it by living your current intention.

Do you have a conscious intention for your life? If so, are you thinking about it, imagining it, feeling it and being as if you already have it?

This is the power of thought over form.

If your current reality is not what you want, and you are identifying only with that, you will continue to create that reality.

Your thoughts have power - they are energy forms. Become aware of when you are focussing on what you don't want, and turn the thought around to what you do want.

Be still and connect with your breath.

Imagine having your desire already manifest.

Feel the feelings of already having it.

Notice your posture, your facial expression and the feelings that exist within you.

Sit for a few minutes enjoying this feeling, and thank the Universe in advance for this manifestation.

Feelings create

How are you feeling? Feelings create vibrations, and vibrations manifest things. So as to manifest what you want, you must envision it until you are in the feeling state of it.

When you are in the feeling state of having your intention, your energy field aligns with the same vibration as the thing you are calling for which attracts it to you.

To have something, you must be as if you already have it. The old saying **fake it till you make it** applies here.

Make time to visualise and feel like you already have your desires.

You don't need to feel this way all the time so as to create - and it is unrealistic to believe that you can be in such a state all the time - but the more you do visualise and feel it, the quicker you draw it to you.

Be still and connect with your breath. Contemplate your recent conversations. Ask yourself the following questions:

When have I spoken words that are unloving?

How can I speak more lovingly?

When do I speak negatively about my life?

How can I speak more positively about my life?

Allow the answers to come, and if there are no answers, know that they will come to you in Divine and perfect timing.

Words

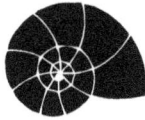

Words have far more power than most of us realise.

Whatever we say or talk about draws to us that of a similar vibration.

Whatever we put out there through our words returns to us.

If you are speaking judgmentally of others, you will also be judged by others. If you are indulging in toxic gossip, you will become the target of toxic gossip. If you are complaining about the **negatives** in your life, you will create more **negatives**.

Conversely, if your words reflect the good you see in others, others will see the good in you.

If you are talking about your life in a positive way, you will draw to you all that is positive.

Everything we say is an affirmation. There are only ever words of love or words of fear. Choose love.

Be still and connect with your breath.

Feel into your heart and ask yourself the following questions:

What would truly fulfill me?

How can I move towards this?

What would be the first step?

Commit to taking the first step.

Successful
people

What is the difference between successful people and unsuccessful people? There are three main differences:

1. Successful people create a vision for themselves based on what they **know** would fulfill them. Unsuccessful people either don't have a vision or they have a vision based on what they **think** will fulfill them.

2. Successful people choose actions and habits that **move towards** their vision. Unsuccessful people do not consciously choose their actions and habits.

3. Successful people **examine and move through** their fears and blocks. Unsuccessful people avoid them.

Lao Tzu told us that the journey of 1,000 miles begins with a single step. The same is true for you and your success.

Be still and connect with your breath.

Feel into your body and feel you present in the here and now.

Know that in this moment you have a choice to respond with a loving thought or a fearful thought.

You have the power to observe your thoughts and choose your thoughts.

Say the following affirmations three times, breathing five times between each:

I am present here now.

I am not my thoughts.

I have the power to observe my thoughts.

I have the power to choose my thoughts.

I choose loving thoughts.

Presence and the Ego

ॐ

Only in presence can you heal, because only in presence you are aware of the fearful ego and your ability to transcend it.

The ego is that part of you who looks at the world through a fearful lens and convinces you that what you see, think and feel is **reality**!

But a negative reality is created by the fearful ego mind and will continue to be created until you gain awareness of it and no longer identify with the fear and lack it engenders.

It is only through presence and awareness that a new reality can be born - one that is full of love, abundance and peace - because in presence you have the ability to choose how you wish to respond to the world.

Be still and connect with your breath.

Feel into your body. Feel you inside yourself.

Say the following affirmations three times, breathing five times between each:

I am I.

I am here for a purpose.

I am unique.

I am I.

You are the treasure

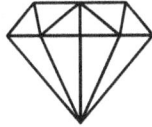

You are searching the world for treasures, but the real treasure is yourself.

You are special and you are unique. In all the world, there is no one quite like you with your special combination of gifts and talents, quirks and oddities.

Embrace your uniqueness!

Do the things you love to do. Become **more of you** and less of anyone else - the old saying "be yourself; everyone else is taken" is true!

Being **you** will make you happy; trying to be like someone else won't. Deepening into **you** and expanding **you** is an act of self-love because you are telling yourself you are worthy of being you.

You are here for one purpose - to simply be you.

Be still and connect with your breath.

Contemplate any relationships where you know you are withholding love.

Visualise the person. Feel into your heart, your centre of love.

Breathe in and out of your heart.

With every breath in, breathe in white light, and with every breath out, imagine your heart opening towards that person.

Say the following affirmation five times, breathing five times between each:

I open my heart to love.

Love everyone

♡

"Love everyone. The poor in spirit, the rich and spoiled, the lost, the proud ... do not argue, get angry or blame them. If you can, try to help them in any way, for being spiritually crippled can be even worse than being physically crippled"
- Leo Tolstoy

When we love others, we feel good in that moment. We don't feel afraid of anything. That's because when we are in the vibration of love, we are truly connected to the Divine Source and with everything else living on Earth. There is nothing to want and nothing to fear when we love.

If you are experiencing a difficult relationship with anybody, ask yourself **What is it in me that is stopping me from loving this person?** It may be judgment, resentment, frustration or unforgiveness. All of these things block love and then create blocks in your life

Let go and choose love and see the good return to you. Only love creates our good, only love heals, only love manifests our desires.

Be still and connect with your breath.

Contemplate any struggles you are currently dealing with.

Say the following affirmation five times, breathing five times between each:

I accept this imperfection, for with it comes more light.

Imperfection

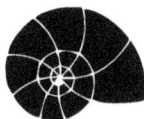

"There's a crack, a crack in everything . That's how the light gets in"
- Leonard Cohen

Let go of the ego's need for perfection.

On the earthy level perfection cannot be attained because we are on a constant journey of growth. We cannot grow and become more without the imperfections of life.

An expectation that things are supposed to be perfect only makes us miserable. **Accept** *that life will never be perfect! Life doesn't need to be perfect.*

There will always be people who rub us up the wrong way or with whom we don't agree, and we will continue to experience events that we don't want and don't like.

Our resistance to these things will only make them worse. Accept them as part of the imperfections of life that, once transcended, ultimately allow more light in.

Be still and connect with your breath.

Contemplate all that you already have.

Say the following affirmations three times, breathing
five times between each:

Everything I need I have.

Everything I need in the future I shall have.

I am open to receive my true abundance today and
always.

True abundance

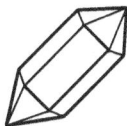

"You will never have enough money to buy all the things you don't need, and you will never have enough time to do all the things you don't really need to do"
- Robert Holden

This really is worth contemplating.

Put another way - what is truly in our highest good we will always have the money or the means to acquire it and the time to do it.

Life really isn't as complicated as we make it. It's the ego that creates lack. It's the ego that creates greed.

When we are balanced and in touch with who we really are, everything we need will flow to us in a Divine and perfect way.

Be still and connect with your breath.

Say the following affirmations five times, allowing five breaths between each:

I let go of all fearful thinking now.

I embrace loving thinking now.

I choose to be in the vibration of peace and love now.

Inner Peace

If there is one thing we must make a priority in our lives, it is inner peace. Inner peace is the fertile soil in which our dreams will grow.

Nothing manifests from fear - except that which we fear. The one and only cause of the fear, worry, anxiety, stress or any other negative emotion we feel is our ego mind.

The ego mind's thoughts create fear.

Inner peace is our natural, original state. If you are not feeling it, examine your thoughts for they will be creating fearful negative emotions.

For every negative loveless thought, there is a positive loving antidote.

Fearful negative thoughts aren't real - they are a creation of the ego mind. All that is love and positivity **is** real. Identify only with love and positivity and see the miracles begin.

Be still and connect with your breath.

Say the following affirmation five times, breathing five times between each:

I am willing to step into the unknown, the field of infinite possibilities.

The Known

The ego loves being in the known, even if the known is lack, boredom or misery.

How many times have you wanted to start something new, and yet so many other things get in the way - the daily chores, other people's needs, errands.

This is your ego sabotaging you and preventing you from going beyond the known. The ego doesn't want you to expand and grow; it wants you to stay stuck.

We must step out of the known if we want our lives to change for the better.

The unknown is the field of all possibilities and where your full potential lies.

Be still and connect with your breath.

Ask yourself the following questions:

Where in my life am I contracting and not expanding?

Why is this?

What am I afraid of?

Acknowledge the fear.

As you breathe in, feel yourself expand.

As you breathe out, let go of all that contracts you. Do this ten times.

Courage

"Life shrinks or expands in proportion to one's courage"
- **Anais Nin**

Be courageous! If you want to live an extraordinary life,
be courageous.

Otherwise you will live a mediocre life, Having courage
doesn't mean that you don't have fear. Having courage
means that you acknowledge your fear and move
through it.

It takes courage to be true to yourself, to withstand
judgement and to take risks. It takes courage to step out
of your comfort zone, to put yourself **out there** and risk
looking like a fool.

It takes courage to speak your truth when you know
that what you're going to say isn't what the other person
wants to hear. It takes courage to be honest with yourself
in difficult circumstances and to ask yourself **what was
my part in this?**

Cultivate courage and watch your life expand!

Be still and connect with your breath. Feel into your body from head to toe.

Imagine a cord dropping down from where you are sitting and descending deep into the earth.

Breathe in the earth energy for ten breaths, and as you breathe out, let go of confusion.

Say the following prayer:

I surrender to You all confusion, and thank You for filling me with Your light and Your clarity.

Continue to focus on the breath until you feel calm and grounded.

Confusion

When you feel confused, remember that confusion doesn't exist **out there**; confusion is created in your own mind.

Confusion happens when your inner state is out of balance, and can be caused by being ungrounded (which creates over-thinking and feeling scattered), not focusing on the right priorities or attempting to take on too much.

So if you're feeling confused, don't try to manage the confusion by trying to fix everything **out there**.

Manage your confusion by re-balancing your inner-state.

Meditate, spend time in nature, take five minutes to feel into your body, focus on your breath and calm your mind.

When inner-balance returns, so does clarity.

Be still and connect with your breath.

Contemplate a situation where you experienced a strong reaction.

Ask yourself:

What was the fear for me in that situation?

Would there be a better way for me to respond? Visualise this response.

Say the following affirmation five times, breathing five times between each:

I am willing to bring more conscious awareness into the experiences that trigger me.

Trigger Reactions

Staying present when an old wound is being triggered isn't easy. Most of us automatically go unconscious and play out our old way of being, and that's what keeps a negative pattern in place.

Every time we react in the same old way, the grooves become deeper.

In presence, we bring a new spacious awareness.

A good way to stay present when you're being triggered is to breathe as soon as you catch yourself in the triggered state.

Breathe in and out deeply and say to yourself **space** - allowing a space between the trigger and the reaction.

This space is where your true power is. In this space you can choose to **respond** and not **react**.

Be still and connect with your breath.

As you breathe, notice that your breath has its own natural pace and rhythm. It is organic and it is innate.

As you align to this natural rhythm, choose to adapt your life to it.

Slow Down

"Perfection is attained by slow degrees. It requires the hand of time."
- Voltaire

Most of us are rushing through life - ticking off the to-do list, thinking we'll be at peace once we've got it all done and erroneously believing that the fast pace we go at will create our success.

Rushing creates stress and attracts to us situations that require more rushing. And if/when we get to where we want to be, we won't be able to relax and enjoy the fruits of our labour, because we have programmed ourselves to rush through that moment too.

Racing through life becomes a pattern unless we recognise it and choose to slow down.

All that is rightfully yours will be yours. Rushing won't bring it to you any quicker; it may even keep it from you. There is no need to rush; no need to panic. By all means, focus and work on your dreams and goals, but smell the roses and enjoy the journey too.

Be still and connect with your breath.

Focus on your heart chakra, your centre of love and compassion.

Say the following affirmation five times, breathing five times between each:

I am doing the best I can and I release all barriers to loving myself more.

Self love and self compassion

The journey towards self-love is not an easy one.

Most of us, on some level, judge, criticise and chide ourselves for not being the person we are **supposed to be**.

Self-compassion is the key.

Being kind to ourselves and reminding ourselves regularly that we are doing the best we can in any given moment.

Most of us haven't been taught how to love ourselves, because our parents didn't know how and society didn't know how.

No wonder it is a struggle! And all the more reason to be self-compassionate.

Be still and connect with your breath.

Breathe in the healing life force energy and imagine it filling your heart.

Picture this as white healing light. Then breathe out, imagining that you are breathing out all that isn't love.

Do this for five minutes and Say the following affirmation five times, breathing five times between each:

I am love.

Loving Others

The more you love yourself, the more you become a magnet for love ... and the more you love others, the more love you feel for yourself. The energy is circular and synergistic.

The basis for attracting true love is finding true love for ourselves, and yet we can find true love for ourselves by giving true love to others - be it people, animals or the earth.

We are here to learn about love. Many of us mistake love for other things - guilt, dependence, neediness. We all get led astray from time to time. I know of no better description of love than this passage from The Book of Corinthians:

Love is patient, love is kind. It does not envy, it does not boast, it is not proud. It does not dishonor others, it is not self-seeking, it is not easily angered, it keeps no record of wrongs. Love does not delight in evil but rejoices with the truth. It always protects, always trusts, always hopes, always perseveres.

It is a wonderful reminder of what love is.

Be still and connect with your breath.

Contemplate your plans, your goals and your dreams.

Connect in with the Divine Source and say the following prayer:

I surrender it all to You and I trust that if this is part of

Your plan for me, it will manifest in Divine and perfect timing.

And it is not, I trust that you will show me the way.

Thank You.

Paradox of life

"Life is what happens while you're busy making other plans"
- **John Lennon**

Yes, by all means make plans.
Yes, by all means be self-determined.
Yes, by all means make a vision for your life.

And yet ...

Surrender it all! Life is a paradox. We are powerful and creative, and yet we are nothing without the Supreme Intelligence.

By surrendering, we are acknowledging that the Universe is ultimately in charge; not us.

We trust that if something gets presented to us that is not what we thought was a part of our plan, it may be that it is!

Don't get so attached to plans that you miss the **big** opportunities and growth experiences (that were never planned) along the way.

Be still and connect with your breath.

Allow yourself to feel any fear-based emotions that are present.

Every feeling needs to be acknowledged; even the fearful ones.

Ask yourself:

What do I need to believe to feel this way?

Sit with the question for five minutes.

An answer may come forth, or it may not.

Trust that if you have asked the question, the answer will present itself to you in Divine and perfect timing.

Suffering

Fear-based emotions create suffering, but suffering can lead to your awakening when you become aware.

Prejudice, anger, selfishness, jealousy, hate, repression, blame, envy, greed, possessiveness, egotism, vengeance, regret, cynicism, indifference, hopelessness, despair and loneliness ... are all fear-based emotions.

All of these fear-based emotions are delusions of the ego mind.

Beneath your fears, you are a fully enlightened, loving soul. You are here to rise above the energy of fear.

Only love is real!

Be still and connect with your breath.

Contemplate any challenge you are struggling with.

As you think about the situation, Say the following affirmation five times, breathing five times between each:

I accept that this situation was created for me by the Universe for my growth and evolution.

Acceptance

Acceptance is forgiving every moment that doesn't go
our way.

It is perceiving everything that happens to us as given to
us by the Divine, both the good and the bad.

With this attitude, we let go of the need to think **why
me?**

Embedded into **every** life will be challenges because we
are here to evolve, and we evolve through challenge.

By accepting our challenges, we no longer lose energy
through resisting them. Instead, we feel a sense of grace
and new levels of understanding become accessible.

Be still and connect with your breath.

If a thought comes up that creates a fearful emotion, ask yourself the following question:

Does this thought serve me?

If the answer is no, choose to change the thought to one that gives you a feeling of peace.

Thought Patterns

Becoming aware of our thought patterns and realising we have the ability to change them, and therefore change our lives, is both empowering and perplexing, because we are constant thinkers.

It can be a difficult concept to accept.

Yet everything begins with a thought. Becoming aware of our thoughts and seeing them just as thoughts, as opposed to believing them to be real, is the first step towards transformation.

Letting go of thoughts that make us feel anxious, unhappy or fearful, and changing them into thoughts that feel loving and peaceful will create a new reality.

The first step is awareness, the next step is to examine the thought, and the next is to ask yourself if this thought serves you. If the answer is no, choose a thought that gives you peace.

Be still and connect with your breath.

Say the following affirmation five times, breathing five times between each:

I honour my past and I am willing to heal my past.

Look Back

"Without freedom from the past, there is no freedom at all."
- **Krishnamurti**

Look back to see where you have come from. When you know where you have come from, you are able to understand where you are and why.

Some of us only want to focus on the future, but if we haven't healed our past, our ideal future cannot be created.

Past, present and future are all intertwined and are all one.

The only time to consider the past is now, and the only time to consider the future is now.

Now is where the magic happens.

Be still and connect with your breath.

Consider your desire to want to fix someone else's problems.

Acknowledge the feelings that come up for you, and your bodily sensations.

Acknowledge any sense of powerlessness or sadness.

As you breathe in, breathe the energy back to yourself.

As you breathe out, let that person and their problems go. Say:

I acknowledge that _____ has all the resources within him/her to live his/her best life. The only person I need to work on is me.

Beware The Fixer

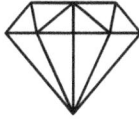

The **fixer** is your ego mind wanting to help, but in a way that won't ever serve you or the other person.

The fixer wants to solve the other person's problem and to make things better, but no one benefits when the fixer is at large.

When we attempt to fix other people's problems, we essentially **steal** their problems.

These problems aren't ours to fix! We deny them of the growth they need to have in order to fix their own problem.

And by focussing on their problem, we ignore our own.

When you feel the need to fix another's problems, take a deep breath in, and bring your energy back to yourself, where it belongs and remind yourself that the other person has all the resources within themselves to fix their own problems.

Know that you can help them most by simply listening and empathising.

Be still and connect with your breath.

Ponder the vision you have for your life.

Picture the final outcome.

Does this give you a feeling of peace?

If not, adjust your vision until you feel peaceful.

Does this lead to peace?

ॐ

Do your goals and dreams lead to more peace in your life?

If they do not, you may want to reconsider them. Inner peace is an important element of true abundance.

If we do not have peace, how can we really appreciate and enjoy our outcomes?

If you are going through a time of great change, you may not be feeling very peaceful. This is normal. Consider the final outcome.

Will this give you more peace?

If your answer is yes, go for it.

Be still and connect with your breath. Ask yourself:

Is there an idea or sense of inspiration that I am denying or blocking from happening?

Sit with this question for a few minutes and if the answer is yes, acknowledge what this is.

Now ask yourself:

What is stopping me from creating this?

When the answer comes, acknowledge it

Say the following affirmation five times, breathing five times between each:

I am willing to create this.

Creative vs. destructive

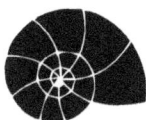

Creativity and destruction are two sides of the same coin. Beware that if you are denying your creativity, you may become destructive instead.

We are all innately creative. We are here to create. What you are here to create will be unique to you and your purpose.

Creativity needs to be expressed. It is one thing to have an idea; it is another to go about its earthly creation. If we deny our creativity, the energy reverses and becomes destructive.

Our frustration can lead to destruction - of self, relationships or other things

Do not deny your creativity! Choose a project and commit to its completion. You will not only achieve a sense of accomplishment; you will achieve a profound energy shift that will take you to another level.

Be still and connect with your breath.

Feel into your body and know that you are an energy field of pure potentiality.

As you breathe in, breathe in unlimited potential, and as you breathe out, let go of all limitations.

Say the following affirmation five times, breathing five times between each:

I now release all limitations and open up to my unlimited potential.

You are unlimited potential

There is a field of unlimited potential and you are a part of it.

Just as a small acorn has the potential to become a fully grown oak tree, you too have within you the ability to reach your full potential. And just as the acorn sprouts and then grows steadily with earth, sunlight and water, so too can your dreams - with steady contribution (working towards your vision), patience and determination.

Don't let your ego mind tell you that your dreams are impossible! Don't put off taking the first step towards creating what you really want, or being the person you really want to be.

Take one step at a time. When you start moving towards what you want, energy shifts, serendipity begins to happen and you will eventually get there. And all because you took that first step! Your full potential already exists within you, and you are here to live it.

Be still and connect with your breath.

If you are yearning for more understanding, feel into the feeling.

Where do you feel it in your body?

Acknowledge your emotions. Ask yourself:

Where am I not seeking to understand others?

Say the following affirmations three times, breathing five times between each:

I am willing to understand others

I am willing to understand myself.

Seek to understand

"Grant that I may not so much seek to be understood, as to understand "
- St Francis of Assisi

So often, we want to be understood, but we don't get the understanding we need. This is our ego focusing on **getting** rather than receiving.

If we are not getting the understanding we need, we must learn to give first what we wish to receive.

Our own pain comes from our needy wounded child, and from this place we become unaware of anyone else's needs but our own. If you want to be understood, make it your priority to seek to understand the other person first.

This takes vulnerability and courage, but when we seek to understand the other first, a miracle occurs.

Our neediness disappears, replaced by compassion and understanding for the other, and greater compassion and understanding for ourselves.

Be still and connect with your breath. Visualise the person you need to forgive.

Notice the feelings that come up for you when you think of the person and what happened.

Notice where you feel these feelings in your body.

Name them if you can (anger, guilt, shame, sadness …)

Say:

I am willing to forgive _____

I am willing to let go of the feelings of

_____

Visualise a cord from your navel that is attached to this person, the event(s) and the feelings. Imagine the cord being cut and the person, event(s) and feelings float away into the light.

Say:

I let this go with love.

You may need to do this process every day until you feel free.

Forgiveness

Forgiveness is imperative if we want to move forward in our lives. A lack of forgiveness poisons us with the toxic emotions of anger, hurt and resentment.

We may push these emotions away so that we don't consciously feel them, but they remain in our energy field and pollute our lives if not processed.

We can rid ourselves of the people who have hurt us, but unless we forgive them, we will meet similar people and circumstances over and over, until we forgive the **original sin**.

This is why forgiving our parents and anyone who wounded us in childhood is key to our freedom.

Forgiveness is not condoning what happened; it is choosing to accept what happened and to let go of the toxic emotions that we hold. We choose to forgive for **ourselves**, not anybody else.

Forgiveness frees us of negative energy and sets us free.

Be still and connect with your breath.

*If you are faced with change or uncertainty, imagine being **the eye of the storm**.*

Be completely still and quiet as you witness the change happening around you.

No matter what is happening, there is always a still, serene place within you that can be accessed.

True security is only to be found within you, not outside of you.

Say the following affirmation five times, breathing five times between each:

In this time of change and uncertainty, I am safe.

Security

True security can only be found from within.

It is normal to want to feel safe and secure - most of us need some level of financial security, emotional security and a sense that we have some control over our lives. And yet, life is full of uncertainty and instability, even in the things we most count on.

We may think we have full control of our lives until we hit a financial crisis, a key relationship breaks down, we lose our job, we or someone close becomes ill.

*Life has a way of showing us that we are never ultimately in control. The **only** thing we have control of is our response to these things, because we **do** have control of our minds if we so choose.*

Learning to accept that life is a process of things forever building up and breaking down, endings and new beginnings, disappointments and miracles, losses and gains helps us to relinquish control.

"Only in growth, reform and change, paradoxically enough, is true security to be found".
*- **Morrow Lindbergh***

Be still and connect with your breath.

As you breathe, become aware of the spaciousness that exists within you.

Become aware of the spaciousness all around you.

In this spaciousness, you have the power to choose Divinely right responses and Divinely right action.

Feel the stillness within you.

From this stillness can emerge Divinely right responses and Divinely right action.

The Ego asserts itself

Beware the need to assert yourself!

*Asserting ourselves often comes from the ego, the **I**, the smallest version of ourselves, that demands to be noticed, to tell others what's right, and to feel superior. This is not true power.*

True power doesn't need to overpower others. True power is not reacting whenever we feel triggered. It comes from knowing that we have a choice in each and every moment as to how we respond.

If you're asserting yourself when you're feeling emotionally triggered, you can be sure your ego is at play, and your assertion won't create a desired outcome.

Don't let your ego mind trick you into thinking that asserting yourself is setting a boundary. It isn't. Boundaries can be set without words and without any input from the ego.

Becoming aware of the ego and its tricky ways comes through practising presence and awareness.

Be still and connect with your breath.

Allow yourself to honour your sense of grief and loss.

Visualise whatever was lost being taken into the Light to transmute into a ball of energy.

Know that this ball of energy is waiting for the Divinely right time to return to you in a positive and loving form.

The law of replacement

"What we have once enjoyed deeply we can never lose.
All that we love deeply becomes a part of us"
- Helen Keller

It is painful to lose something we value or someone we
love, but it's even more painful if we have a strong belief
system in loss.

There is a Universal Law called The Law of Replacement.
Energy never disappears; it only ever transforms.
Because we are constantly evolving for the better,
whatever we lose will be replaced by something either the
same or better.

If you have experienced a loss - be it a job, money,
relationship or anything else - remind yourself of this
Law.

Know that it will be replaced in Divine and perfect timing
with something the same or better. Of course, you must
allow yourself to grieve the loss, but know there is a
bigger picture and light at the end of the tunnel.

Be still and connect with your breath.

Feel yourself present in the here and now.

Feel into your body and sense your full potential right now.

Say the following affirmation five times, breathing five times between each:

I live my full potential now.

Potentiality

It is only in presence that you can be in your full potential. Your full potential is not an abstract concept that waits somewhere in your future.

Your full potential exists **now**.

Embrace your full potential, right here, right now by being fully in the present moment and doing everything mindfully and well, even if it is not what you ultimately want to be doing.

This very way of being - present and doing your best - will take you to where you want to be.

You cannot reach your full potential in the future unless you live your full potential in the now!

Be still and connect with your breath.

Say the following affirmation five times, breathing five times between each:

I am willing to transcend my current reality and open up to infinite possibilities.

Infinite Possibilities

Our world contains infinite possibilities, but most of us see only a fraction of these possibilities available to us, as we see life through a filter of limitations.

This filter was created from the self-limiting beliefs we have been given from our ancestors, parents, peers, the media and the world in general.

Just because our mind cannot see these infinite possibilities, doesn't mean they don't exist.

*Be willing to know that there are infinite possibilities for you and your life, which your conditioned mind cannot see, and that your current reality **can** be transcended.*

Be still and connect with your breath.

As you breathe in, breathe in healing light.

Feel the Universal energy all around you.

Know that this energy is encoded with Divine and perfect timing.

Breathe out and let go of your need to control timing.

Say the following affirmation five times, breathing five times between each:

I live fully in the now and I allow the future to take care of itself.

Patience

Patience isn't about waiting. Patience is accepting that the Universe manifests in Divine and perfect timing, not the timing of the ego.

Success is created by a culmination of good decisions and habits that are in alignment with what we want, made over a period of time.

"People tend to overestimate what they can do in the short term, and underestimate what they can do in the long term".
- Bill Gates

Be still and connect with your breath.

Contemplate any areas of your life where you are minding someone else's business.

As you breathe in, bring your energy back to yourself.

As you breathe out, let go of the other person's business and return it to them.

Mind your own business

Whose business are you in? Yours or somebody else's?

If you have a habit of getting into other people's business - becoming overly involved in their problems, holding their **stuff**, checking up on them, trying to fix their problems or needing to control them - you will drain your own energy and lose yourself.

Not minding your own business isn't good for others and it certainly isn't good for you.

By being overly involved in their lives, you rob other people of autonomy and sovereignty, and you rob yourself of your own presence and energy.

You essentially abandon yourself.

If your energy is being directed where it shouldn't be, bring your energy back to yourself and your own business

Be still and connect with your breath.

Contemplate the things you worry about that are beyond your control.

As you breathe in, breathe in Light.

As you breathe out, let go of those things that you cannot control.

Do this for a few minutes. Feel yourself lighter and freer.

Say the Serenity Prayer:

God, grant me the serenity to accept the things I cannot change.

Courage to change the things I can.

And the wisdom to know the difference.

Control

There are some things that are within our control and others that aren't. We can create a lot of misery for ourselves when we worry about the things that are beyond our control.

We cannot control other people's moods or choices. We cannot control the weather. We cannot control certain outcomes. Putting energy into these things is a waste. Worrying about what we cannot control is using the Universal Law of Attraction in a negative way.

The Serenity Prayer is a powerful prayer -

God, grant me the serenity to accept the things I cannot change.

Courage to change the things I can.

And the wisdom to know the difference.

When you do begin to know the difference, you will no longer waste time, energy and emotions on those things you cannot change, and instead focus your energies on those things you can. You will feel lighter, freer and happier.

Be still and connect with your breath. Ask:

Where is my life lacking balance?

Sit with the question and allow the answers to come forth.

And now ask yourself:

How can I achieve more balance?

If an answer doesn't come, have faith that it will present itself to you in Divine and perfect timing.

Balance

If you've ever been sailing, finding balance is a bit like finding that sweet spot in the sail - just the right amount of tautness against the wind will move you forward.

We learn balance through getting out of balance.

Working so hard that we forget to have a personal life; being so attached to an outcome that we forget to relax and enjoy the moment; getting so involved in a relationship that we begin to lose our sense of self.

Life has a way of showing us where we need to learn balance.

Be still and connect with your breath.

Feel into your body for a minute so as to get out of your thinking mind.

Feel yourself present in the here and now, and remind yourself that **nothing** is that important if it means feeling that you're struggling.

What are the thoughts that are driving your feelings of stress and struggle?

Observe the thoughts that are creating your stress and struggle, and say the following prayer:

I surrender to You my thoughts of stress and struggle.

Please replace these thoughts with thoughts of peace and love.

Thank You.

Stress and struggle

Struggling, battling, pushing, forcing are all a waste of time.

Whatever we create out of stress and struggle will contain the seeds of stress and struggle.

If there any areas in your life where you feel stressed and struggling, **stop!**

Take a few deep breaths.

Your ego mind may tell you that if you just keep trying, forcing, stressing and struggling, then you'll be rewarded with an answer, achievement or solution but nothing could be further from the truth!

This inner state will only create further stress and struggle.

The best results always come from a peaceful mind.

Be still and connect with your breath.

Contemplate your current difficulty.

Choose now to see it as an opportunity to grow and evolve.

Say the following prayer:

I surrender this difficulty to You.

Thank You for releasing me from any old life strategies that no longer serve me.

Thank You for downloading to me the necessary new life strategies that are needed.

Breathe out, surrender and have faith.

Life Strategies

It takes awareness to realise how we operate. Many of our life strategies come from our childhood. Some come later as we grow into new experiences. Strategies we learned then may not work now, and they are not meant to, because we are here to evolve and grow. We are not meant to stay the same. Our soul will create the very challenges we need to transcend the old strategy.

You will know an old life strategy isn't working for you anymore if you're no longer getting the results you used to get, if you're experiencing difficulty over and over in a certain area of your life, or if you are feeling worn out, angry, frustrated or resentful on a regular basis.

Einstein told us that no problem could be resolved by the same energy that was used to create it, and yet that is often what we attempt to do - resolve the problem with the strategy that created it in the first place.

Be still and connect with your breath.

Sit with an issue where you are not sure how to respond.

Ask yourself:

What am I meant to learn here?

Is it to accept and tolerate?

Or is it to take action and communicate?

Allow the answer to emerge and then follow that truth.

Active vs. Passive

In any relationship - be it with your partner, friend, boss, mother, father, sibling - there are times to be passive and times to be active, and it takes intuitive wisdom to know which approach to take.

Some problems are best left alone to sort themselves out, while others need to be addressed and a solution proactively found.

How to know the difference? If a problem is ongoing or keeps recurring over and over again and you don't want to deal with it again and again, then it is time to be proactive!

It is human nature to like our comfort zone but we can get stuck in the ever-repeating known. Problems are the Universe telling us **it's time to grow!**

Sometimes our growth lesson is simply to let go and allow, and to learn tolerance and at other times it is to actively seek change. If you're not sure whether to be active or passive, sit with it awhile.

Be still and connect with your breath.

Contemplate a current problem.

Say the following prayer:

I surrender this problem to You.

(Visualise handing the problem over)

May Your Divine Intelligence come through me.

May this problem be resolved in Divine and perfect timing.

Thank You.

Solutions

There really is a solution to every problem ... but so often we don't find it because we're too busy trying to **work it out** with our mind. The mind is a wonderful calculator - it can do maths, sort and organise ... but it is a very limited tool when it comes to the more complicated issues of life.

There is a Divine Matrix of Supreme Intelligence available to us always and it already has the solution to every problem. We can all access this Intelligence through stillness and meditation.

If you have a problem, surrender it to the Universe. Ask for a solution, then **trust** and be ready for the solution to come. It may come to you through a dream, a sign, an idea, a hunch, a song or Divine synchronicity .

Stay aware and be ready!

Be still and connect with your breath.

Consider the scenario you fear. Ask yourself:

What is the worst that could happen?

And then what?

And then what?

And then what?

Keep asking this question. Observe and acknowledge your fear.

As you breathe in, breathe in love, and as you breathe out, breathe out fear. Do this ten times.

Fearing the worst

♡

When a misfortune threatens, consider seriously what is the very worst that could possibly happen.

Having looked any possible misfortune in the face, give yourself sound reasons as to why it would not be such a terrible disaster - and such reasons do exist. It is the ego mind that catastrophises, fears loss and judges situations as **disastrous**.

When you can get to the stage of acceptance that your fear could come to pass and you would still be ok, you will find inner peace.

Worry and anxiety is the energy that will create the thing you fear.

Acceptance, on the other hand, actually lessens its likelihood.

Be still and connect with your breath.

If you feel enmity towards anyone, say the following prayer:

I surrender to you my need for an enemy

Please fill me with Your Light

Please help me to see him/her as You see him/her

May I see them through Your eyes of love.

Enemies

To hate another is to hate oneself. We all live within the one Universal Mind. What we think about another we think about ourselves.

We cannot have an outside enemy, unless there is an enemy within!

If you have an enemy, forgive them. Ask to be filled with Light to dissolve all bitterness and resentment, because the one who is being harmed is you.

When we choose forgiveness, and show goodwill, all good returns to us and enhances our lives in wonderful ways.

Be still and connect with your breath.

Say the following affirmations three times, breathing five times between each:

I expect love

I expect success

I expect good health

I expect to abundance

I expect miracles

I allow the Universe to deliver this to me in its own unique way.

Expectations

Are you expecting things to go right or things to go wrong?

Watch your thoughts and your words. Think and speak as if all will be well, and at the same time detach yourself from outcomes.

Even if something doesn't go the way you specifically want it to, know that the Universe is on your side.

The Universe is forever propelling you towards your highest good and whatever happens will ultimately be perfect, even if you don't know it yet.

The Universe works in wondrous ways we know not of!

Be still and connect with your breath.

Ask yourself if there is anything or anyone you are chasing.

Notice how you feel in your body.

You may feel a sense of anxiety.

Say the following affirmations three times, breathing five times between each:

I release the need to chase anything or anyone.

I am open to receive all that is Divinely mine.

Chase
Nothing

Chase nothing - no person, no thing, no outcome.

The more you chase something, the more it eludes you.
And yet if you let it go, very often it will present itself to
you with little effort.

That is because what is Divinely yours will come to you
if you allow it, and you allow it through letting go and
surrendering. That which is not Divinely yours won't
come to you.

And so it follows that those who reject you are not for
you. Rejection is the Universe protecting you!

By all means, apply for that job, contact that person,
send that message - but then let go and let the Universe
do the work.

Be still and connect with your breath.

Feel into your body. How do you feel?

If you feel peaceful and happy, you are in the vibration of love. If you feel anxious, angry or sad, you are in the vibration of fear.

Call upon the White Healing Light to fill you from head to toe.

Visualise this healing light clearing away all fear, sending it down deep into Mother Earth.

Say the following affirmation five times, breathing five times between each:

I now release all that isn't love.

And now imagine the White Healing Light is filling you with love.

Say:

All that I do, I do with love.

Do it
with Love

♡

There really is no point in doing anything unless we do it with love!

Love creates wonderful outcomes while fear won't create anything worthwhile.

We are only ever in one of two vibrations - love or fear.

What vibration is leading you? Love or fear?

Be still and connect with your breath.

Contemplate what you are resisting. Say:

The Universe has ever-flowing energy, and therefore I
have ever-flowing energy.

Visualise the Universal energy flowing through you
from head to toe, replenishing you with energy you may
have lost through resistance.

Allow this energy to flow and know that within this
constant flow of energy, you have all the resources within
you to master any situation.

Resistance

Sometimes we have to do things we don't want to do, see people we don't want to see, fulfill an obligation that feels too hard.

The very thought of it drains our energy! So we've got to change the way we think about it.

By proactively accepting the situation, rather than resisting hit, we step into alignment with it, and it's far more likely to go well from that vibration.

Alternatively, we can stay in resistance to it and continue the struggle.

If there's something you've got to do but don't want to do it, take a deep breath of acceptance.

Be still and connect with your breath.

Focus on your heart chakra at the centre of your chest.

This is your balancing chakra.

With every breath in, breathe in healing white light, and with every breath out, let go of any imbalance.

Say the following prayer:

Thank You for clearing in me all imbalance,

Thank You for bringing balance back to my body, mind and spirit.

Extremes

The answer isn't more or less, it's balance.

The ego mind has a way of thinking in extremes, yet
extreme thinking won't resolve anything for long. In
order to bring healing into our lives, we must think and
act in ways that bring balance, such as:

I can take time out for myself, and I can be social

I can be intimate with my partner, and I can have space

I can be generous with my time and money, but I can also
hold back

I can work hard, and I can also have rest

I can feel happy and joyful, and I can feel sad.

There is a time for everything under heaven. Aim for
balance in all things.

Be still and connect with your breath.

Ask yourself:

*Is there any area in my life where I would like to say **no** but feel unable to say it?*

And now ask:

What is the fear if I say no?

Examine the fear. And now, if you feel ready say:

*I am willing to say **no**.*

*Visualise white healing light streaming through your entire body, releasing all that prevents you from saying **no**.*

Learn to
say no

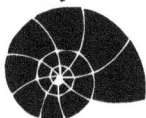

No is not necessarily a negative word; it is a powerful word.

When you are clear about what you want, you will be clear about what you don't want.

Allowing what you don't want into your life will work against you. Many of us were told that it was bad or rude to say **no**. Pleasers find it hard to say **no**.

But here is the problem if you never say **no** to what you don't want:

You will keep being sent more of what you don't want! When we say **no** to what we don't want, the Universe heeds our call, and changes what's being sent.

Be discerning!

Learn to say **no**.

Be still and connect with your breath.

Feel you inside yourself and acknowledge that you are the most important person in your life.

Contemplate the following questions:

Whose approval am I seeking?

Whose approval did I seek when I was young?

How does this relate to now?

Say the following affirmation five times, breathing five times between each:

I release the need for others' approval and I choose to approve of myself.

Seeking approval

Let go of the need for approval from others ...

Needing someone else's approval will ensure that you
will never fully know yourself because you're too busy
pleasing someone else.

Wherever we are seeking approval, we will be giving
away our power to the person whose approval we seek.

Seeking someone's approval comes from the wounded
child who didn't get enough approval earlier in life.

Let go and come back to yourself! The only approval you
need is your own.

Be still and connect with your breath.

Allow your goal or desire to come to mind. Ask yourself:

Am I moving towards or away from this?

If the answer is **away from** or if you get a sense of standing still or going around in circles, ask yourself:

What actions can I take that move me towards my desire?

Commit to taking that action.

Where are you going?

"If you do not change direction, you will end up where you are going"
- Lao Tzu

*Are you clear where you are heading? Some of us live life in **default mode**, unconscious of where we are heading. This will either keep us going round and round in circles or heading in a random direction.*

Some of us head in the direction of A, when we really need to be going in the direction of B.

Our decisions are powerful - once we make a decision, the Universe conspires to make it happen, as long as we also play our part by moving towards our dream and not away from it.

Choose thoughts, words and actions that take you in the right direction!

Be still and connect with your breath.

Ask yourself:

How much love and abundance am I willing to allow?

Ask yourself:

How am I getting in my own way?

Reflect on these questions, and then say the following affirmation five times, breathing five times between each:

I am willing to allow in more love, success and abundance. I am willing to get out of my own way!

Glass Ceiling

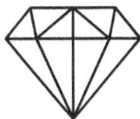

There can be no glass ceiling **out there** unless there is a glass ceiling **within**.

Why do we create a glass ceiling and how can we break through it?

We all have a comfort zone, and it's based on the known. Even if the known is boring, limiting or even toxic, it feels safe; as opposed to the unknown, which holds fear for many of us.

Whatever environment we grew up in, we tend to re-create at an unconscious level. So if we experienced hardship or a limited amount of happiness in our early years, we are likely to keep re-creating that.

Have you ever found yourself feeling joyful, successful and optimistic, only to sabotage this with thinking **yes, but** and turned to thinking of a potential worry? That is your mind creating its own glass ceiling.

Become aware of when you sabotage your happiness, success or abundance with fearful thinking.

Be still and connect with your breath.

Ponder where in your life you believe there is not enough.

Acknowledge that this belief in lack comes from the ego mind, and it has created lack in your life.

Say the following affirmations three times, breathing five times between each:

I now release the vibration of lack.

I am willing to believe in abundance.

The Universe is abundant and therefore I am abundant.

Visualise golden light pouring down on you from Heaven.

There is enough

Our physical world is skewed towards the negative and the concept of lack.

Many of us have experienced **not enough** and we have been conditioned to think in terms of **not enough**.

The ego mind believes there will never be enough of anything - be it money, time, love or achievement - this concept of lack can invade every area of our life!

Every time we say or think that there's not enough of something, it's an affirmation that creates more lack.

Become aware of thoughts and words of lack. These thoughts and words create that reality.

In Divine Mind, there is only abundance.

Be still and connect with your breath.

Become aware of yourself right here, right now in meditation.

Honour yourself in this moment for being present and aware.

Forgive yourself for the times that you have been unaware.

Remind yourself that you are doing the best you can.

Say the following affirmation five times, breathing five times between each:

I am willing to become more aware.

In and out of awareness

Awareness happens when the observer in us is watching.

How often do you have moments of awareness?
Moments where rather than being **in** the movie of your
life, you are the observer of it.

And moments when, rather than being totally **in** your
thoughts, you have the ability to see them for what they
are - just thoughts!

This is a powerful place to be, because from here
we realise that nothing - no person, no thought, no
circumstance - actually has any power over us.

We have the ability to respond and not react, to change a
thought if it doesn't feel good and to choose love over fear
in any situation.

But be kind to yourself - don't expect that you can always
be aware because you've not been conditioned that way.
There will be times when you are aware and times when
you won't be.

Be still and connect with your breath.

Contemplate how you feel about yourself when life isn't going your way.

Say the following affirmation five times, breathing five times between each:

Even though (name the negative circumstances), I choose to love and approve of myself completely and unconditionally.

Self-love starts with self-like

♡

Are you loving yourself only conditionally? Most of us love ourselves:

when we achieve a goal
when we are looking good and feeling fit
when we feel in control of our lives
when we manifest something we want
when other people are praising or appreciating us.

But what about those other times when we fail, when we don't like what we see in the mirror, when life feels out of control and when we feel invisible?

These are the very times that we need to love ourselves more, and not less.

Learning to love yourself unconditionally is learning to like yourself first.

Be still and connect with your breath.

Take a few minutes to think of all you have to be grateful for now.

And then visualise what you desire in the future.

Say the following affirmation five times, breathing five times between each:

I am so grateful for all that I have now, and grateful for all that I shall have in the future.

Here and there

There is no better than **here**!

Don't let your ego mind fool you that once you get **over there** and reach your goal, you'll be happier than you are now.

If you're not happy in your current circumstances, you're unlikely to be happy when you get what you want.

The more positive and grateful you feel right now, the more likely you are to attract those things you desire to you.

No matter how dire things may appear, be grateful. Keep it general and keep it simple if you have to, but this is the best way to be happy, even when you haven't yet realised your desires.

Be still and connect with your breath.

Reflect on the following questions:

In what ways am I seeking attention or wanting to be noticed?

Where in my life do I feel the need to talk myself up?

Am I putting my image before my authentic self?

Say the following prayer:

I surrender to You all that is not humble within me

Thank You for clearing in me all pride and greed.

And for bringing me to the place of humility.

Stay humble

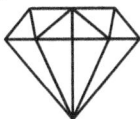

Many of us equate being **humble** with being **less than**, **powerless** and even **poor**, but this isn't true.

The great spiritual leaders - Buddha, Jesus, Lao Tzu and many more - were powerful people who remained humble.

Being humble doesn't mean that you cannot aspire to your dreams and success. It doesn't mean that you cannot live an abundant life.

Being humble means keeping your ego in check, not seeking kudos, letting go of greed and putting people before money.

Being humble requires us to work on substance and not image, to refrain from boasting and seeking attention, and to give purely for the sake of giving.

Pride cometh before a fall. Stay humble and you will not fall.

Be still and connect with your breath.

Bring to mind a person or a situation that is causing you pain or hardship, whether past or present, which you are struggling to accept.

Say the following affirmations three times, breathing five times between each:

Even though I don't know why, I accept that on a soul level, I chose this experience for my growth.

I let go of all judgment of the situation and the people involved.

I am willing to forgive everyone and everything.

I am open to the lessons from this situation.

I am willing to grow from this situation.

We create every situation

On a soul level, we create everything that happens to us. No matter what it is, we have created the spiritual ideal that we require for our soul growth.

The lessons we need are contained within the situation, and the only way to obtain the growth from the experience is to go through it.

How long we suffer depends on how long we want to hang out in victim consciousness. At some point, we must be willing to accept and forgive.

Forgiveness is a process - particularly if we have experienced trauma, heartbreak, loss or betrayal. But in the long-run, not forgiving causes us further pain and will re-create circumstances requiring forgiveness.

When we can fully accept that **we** created the situation for our soul's growth, we arrive at a level that enables us to understand and grow.

Be still and connect with your breath.

Ask yourself:

What is one positive thing I have because of (name the body issue)?

Say:

I am so grateful for (name the positive).

Consciously send love (whether it is yours or the Universe's love) to your body.

Say the following affirmations five times, breathing five times between each:

I am willing to love my body.

Your body

The relationship you have with your body will create either wellness and beauty, or disease and unattractiveness.

Your body wants to be loved. If you're not liking what you see in the mirror, chances are that you won't be feeling a lot of love for your body.

And if you are ill, it is likely that you are **hating** your illness.

The only vibration that heals is love!

Begin by looking for at least one positive aspect of your physical appearance or your disease and give gratitude.

The more you can focus lovingly on these positives, the more you will be shown, and the more grateful you will feel. It just starts with that first step.

Be still and connect with your breath.

Contemplate any area of your life where you are lacking trust.

Say the following prayer:

I surrender to You my fear and insecurity

I surrender to You my need to control this situation

I now release all barriers to trusting in You

And knowing I am safe always.

Trusting others

"The best way to find out if you can trust someone is to trust them."
- **Ernest Hemingway**

We can waste a lot of energy not trusting someone - wondering what they are doing, sneaking a look at their phone, attempting to **catch them out**.

If someone is going to betray you, they will do it, and no amount of checking, nagging or spying will stop them. Our ego mind will tell us that by being vigilant, we won't be hurt. This is a lie. In fact these very behaviours will assist in the manifestation of any potential betrayal.

The best way to know if you can trust someone is to trust them. People show their true colours soon enough. We cannot control the outcome.

To have trust, we must trust that the Universe is on our side and will always look after us. This doesn't mean we won't ever experience being hurt, but it does mean that we intrinsically know that no matter what happens, we will always be safe.

Be still and connect with your breath. Feel into your body and acknowledge your body.

As you do this, acknowledge your body's innate wisdom. Feel the wisdom that exists in every cell of your body.

Say the following affirmations three times, breathing five times between each:

Every cell in my body is full of love, wisdom and intelligence

My body keeps me in optimum health.

Give thanks to your body for its wisdom and power.

Healing

We all have the power to heal ourselves.

Your body has an innate intelligence that can tell you
what it needs and when, and it has the ability to create its
own balance and beauty.

If you struggle to believe this, it's not your fault because
we have all been conditioned to think otherwise.

If you are ill, by all means seek medical advice, but also
trust in your body's innate ability to process, detoxify and
heal.

Be still and connect with your breath.

Take a few minutes to explore where you may be holding onto any sense of morality or self-righteousness.

Breathe in the healing life force energy and then breathe out and let go of morality, judgment and self-righteousness.

Do this at least ten times.

Morality

Morality takes all the fun out of life.

Beware of morality - which lurks in the socially conditioned mind. Morality sees others and ourselves as right or wrong, good or bad, sinful or virtuous, acceptable or unacceptable. Morality leads to self-righteousness and we only have to look at history to know where that takes us.

It is a harsh judge that views life through a black and white lens, but life is mostly shades of grey.

These judgements that we apply to ourselves or to others keep us from seeing the beauty within ourselves and them. If we are in judgement, we have shut down our hearts, and from this place, we cannot see the truth.

Let go of the unspoken rules of morality, for truth and peace cannot be found there.

Be still and connect with your breath.

Breathe in and out of your heart, and send love and compassion to yourself.

Feel the spaciousness within your body.

Imagine your entire being now being filled with white healing light.

This light is cleansing you of all ego-driven desires, and bringing you back into balance with your True Self.

Continue to focus on your breath while the white healing light does its work.

Beware
the Ego

Life has a way of showing us where we are holding delusions of ego.

Finding ourselves feeling humiliated, not good enough or belittled can be a reminder that our ego has taken over and has taken a bruising. Only the ego can feel diminished. The True You cannot.

Whenever we are feeling competitive, comparing ourselves to others or feeling the need for recognition or to be heard or noticed, we are allowing our ego to take over.

To correct this inclination, give yourself an assignment to be as much in the background as you can for a day (or even better, a week!).

Notice your need to assert yourself, to get attention or to push your point of view or give advice, and don't act on it. Make a commitment to be interested in others, to listen to them and to allow them to shine. Be soft and gentle and consciously allow others the right to expand.

Be still and connect with your breath.

Contemplate your current challenge.

Sit with the question:

How can I make this situation more acceptable and enjoyable?

You may get an answer; you may not.

You've asked the question so trust that the answer will come in Divine and perfect timing.

Not what
but how

Many of us face situations that for various reasons we cannot leave - a job, a relationship, a family challenge, illness, loneliness.

In such situations, the only way to achieve a sense of relief is to accept the circumstances and to change our attitude towards the circumstances.

If we are looking at our circumstances through the lens of scarcity - focusing on what's wrong and not on what's right, if we are feeling resentful, if we are waking up dreading the day instead of giving gratitude and putting forth our positive intentions, our circumstances will remain the same or even get worse.

It's not what you do but how you do it! Choosing to focus on the good - giving gratitude for the little things, choosing a loving vibration and continuing to visualise and imagine those things you do want - will not only improve your current circumstances; it will create your ideal future.

Be still and connect with your breath.

Say the following affirmations three times, breathing
five times between each:

It is good for my mind, body and spirit to relax.

I give myself permission to relax.

I am worthy and deserving of relaxation.

Relaxation

Beware the ego mind that likes to keep you running on a program called **busy**.

When you endeavour to relax, it will have you think **I should be doing something** or **I'm wasting time** or **I'm not achieving**.

If you've been busy lately, give yourself permission to take some time off and relax.

By taking time out to relax and just be, you give yourself time to recharge - your creativity will increase and you will feel revitalised by a newfound sense of purpose and inspiration.

Your ego mind may tell you that you don't have time to relax but your soul knows that relaxation time is its fuel.

Your wellbeing is of the utmost importance. Without it, nothing else really matters.

Be still and connect with your breath.

Contemplate any criticism you have received from others and ask yourself:

Do I in any way agree with this criticism?

Is there any truth in it for me?

Is there anything I can learn from it?

How can I use this criticism to activate positive change for myself?

Send gratitude to the person who criticised you and let them go with love.

Criticism

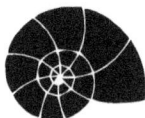

If we are dealing with criticism, we are probably already criticising ourselves for the same things we are being criticised for. Criticism from the outside cannot be happening without it happening already on the inside.

Sometimes there can be an element of helpful truth in criticism, but because we cloud our minds with shame, we feel unable to see it and receive it.

Be willing to examine criticism and to see it in a helpful, rather than a fearful way.

Then you can choose to take on board what feels truthful and make positive changes accordingly, and let go of criticism that feels untruthful.

And at the same time, remind yourself that we all have faults and we are all lovable.

Be still and connect with your breath.

Think of a situation that is causing you stress.

Ask yourself the following:

Am I looking at this situation through the filter of shame or the truth that I am enough?

Am I looking at this situation through the filter of scarcity or the truth of abundance?

Am I looking at this situation through the filter of fear or the truth of love?

Am I looking at this situation through the filter of resistance or the truth of acceptance?

Filters

What we see is not necessarily what is true, because we all have **filters** - wounds, beliefs and conditioning that alter our perception.

When anything happens, that event goes through a filter of beliefs and past experiences.

If we don't challenge how we think about it, we may not be seeing it clearly or making the most of it.

What we think about something determines how we feel and how we respond.

Be still and connect with your breath.

Bring to mind the incompletion. Ask yourself:

Do I wish to complete this?

If the answer is no, then complete this by closing it. If the answer is yes, ask yourself:

What is stopping me from completing this?

Allow the answer to emerge.

Say the following prayer:

I surrender this incompletion to You

Thank You for providing me with all that I need

To complete this.

Incompletion

Do you have tasks that have not been completed?
Do you have things to say that have not been said?
Do you have plans that never get materialised?

Whatever is left incomplete in your life is an energy drain. Tasks or creative pursuits that we don't finish stay in our psyche, hovering in the background.

Every time we see them, our energy drains a little more until we get them done. Conversations we would like to have, but don't, repeat themselves over and over in our minds, draining more energy.

*Thoughts such as **I must finish that** or **I'm going to do that when I get time** further drain our energy.*

If you have anything incomplete in your life, make a practical plan to complete it. Notice the feeling when you complete each task. The sense of satisfaction and inner peace is your energy being restored.

Be still and connect with your breath.

Consciously acknowledge any toxic emotions you feel at present.

If you can, name them.

Observe them. Say hello to them.

Do not try to push them away.

When you feel ready, let them go.

Mastering emotions

Our emotions create everything. Some say our thoughts do, but it is the emotions that spring from those thoughts that creates.

And it therefore follows that the more we can control our emotions, the more able we are to manifest. Some emotions are not easy to master - anger, jealousy, envy to name a few.

If we are feeling these emotions on a regular basis, we will keep creating more situations that are opportunities for us to heal these emotions. So if you're angry, you will keep creating situations that anger you.

How do we learn to master our emotions? Firstly, it's not by ignoring them or pretending they are not there (otherwise known as denial or repression).

All emotions need to be acknowledged and felt. We can feel it, observe it, acknowledge it and then consciously choose to let it go.

Be still and connect with your breath.

Imagine now a mist of pink healing energy pouring down on you - this is the Universe's love. The Universe loves you completely and unconditionally.

With every breath in, breathe in this pink healing light and allow it to fill you from head to toe.

Open yourself to the loving intent of the Universe.

Know now that you **are** love..

Say the following affirmation five times, breathing five times between each:

I am always loved.

Seeking love

We all need love. From the time we were born, we have depended upon it for our survival.

However, the need for love can sometimes drive love away. Most of us believe that we must have love from other people in order to feel loved, but this is not true.

Love comes from the Source, and you can access this through being present, being in nature, nurturing yourself, prayer and meditation.

This is yet another reason to start a meditation practice, for it is the most powerful way to be present and to feel love, The more love we feel within us, the more love we attract to us from the outside.

If we are seeking love from an empty place, it will evade us.

Love must begin with us.

Be still and connect with your breath.

Visualise the person with whom you have difficulty.

Ask yourself:

What good do I see in this person?

Consciously send that person your love.

Say the following prayer:

I surrender to You all that isn't love for this person.

Thank You for allowing only love to remain.

Look for the good

If you are experiencing difficulty with anyone, look for the good in that person.

Even the most difficult or dislikable person has some good in them! Leave the rest for the Universe to deal with.

Whatever we focus on becomes greater, and whatever we take our focus away from diminishes - that is a Universal law.

The more you focus on that person's positive aspects, you change your vibration into love, and the other person will feel a difference energetically when they are with you.

This may or may not change how they respond to you - but the outcome is not the point.

The point is that you have made a shift towards unconditional love, and by doing this, you heal yourself and create good karma.

Be still and connect with your breath.

Contemplate your obligations and as each one arises, ask yourself:

Am I doing this out of fear or love?

If the answer is fear, ask yourself:

What is the fear if I don't do this?

Say the following prayer:

I surrender this fear to You.

Please fill me with your Light, so that I may choose from love, and not fear.

Thank You.

Obligations

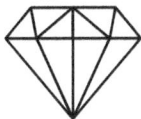

Most of us have obligations - to go to work, to parent, to help a loved one when they are ill - but we can over-obligate ourselves.

There is a difference between a healthy obligation and an unhealthy one. A healthy obligation is one that we choose because it is aligned with our values and has meaning and importance to us.

This obligation comes from love.

An unhealthy obligation is one where we feel that we **should** but don't really want to, and if we don't do it, we fear judgment and criticism. In these circumstances, you will hear yourself saying **I have to** or **I should**.

This is an obligation based on fear, and ultimately no good will come of it.

Consider carefully before committing to a new obligation. Take back your power, be true to yourself and make choices out of love. Ultimately, you will feel a lot better for it.

Be still and connect with your breath.

Consider any hurt you are holding from words or actions that were directed towards you.

Say:

Return to sender.

Visualise the energy of what was done or said returning to the sender and visualise white healing light pouring through you, releasing all effects of the words or action.

Return to sender

Here are three very helpful words to say to yourself if someone says or does something to you that is hurtful or not wanted - **Return to sender**.

Imagine their words or action turning around and going right back at them, because, in truth, they actually will be (hence those wise Biblical words - **Do unto others as you would wish them do unto you**).

Whatever we give out we receive.

By doing this simple inner exercise, you are also energetically propelling the words or deed away from you, and not taking them on and being hurt by them.

We have no control over what others choose to do, but we do have control of what we choose to do about it.

Be still and connect with your breath.

Contemplate your desires, and ask yourself:

What am I prepared to give up for it?

What am I likely to have to give up for it?

*Sit with this realisation and if it feels acceptable,
continue with your intention.*

There is a price to pay

There is a price to pay for everything, be it time, money, energy or something else.

This is because energy cannot be created and it cannot die; it transmutes.

If you want to manifest something, consider carefully what you may have to give up for it.

Otherwise you may not like it when the bill becomes due.

If something or someone disappears in your life, be aware that this may be the Universe making space for a new manifestation that you have been wanting.

Be still and connect with your breath.

Feel into your body and feel you inside yourself. Ask yourself:

How am I feeling?

What do I need right now?

What am I prepared to give to others?

What am I not prepared to give to others?

How do I know when I've given too much?

How do I create healthy boundaries that protect my energy?

Allow time for the answers to come.

Put yourself first

Sometimes the demands of others and our own confused expectations of ourselves can create a big complicated mess.

If you find that the needs of others are beginning to affect you in a negative way, stand back and take time out for yourself, because if you aren't clear and energised, you will be of no help to yourself or anybody else.

Make your sense of inner peace and happiness your number one priority, and ultimately everybody else will benefit.

Be still and connect with your breath.

Contemplate if there are any relationships in your life where you are not feeling respected. Ask yourself:

What part have I played in creating this?

How can I change my part in it?

Say the following prayer:

I surrender this situation to You.

Thank You for filling me with Your Light.

And clearing me of all that is preventing me from respecting myself.

We teach others how to treat us

We teach others how to treat us by showing them what we will put up with and what we won't.

Most of us have moments of behaving in ways we regret later, and a loving heart will seek to understand and forgive. If however, the occasional moments of regrettable behaviour from a loved one become an ongoing pattern, we must ask ourselves why we are putting up with it.

Poor or abusive behaviour can build up over time, and the recipient can become like the proverbial frog who slowly and unknowingly boils to death as the water it is swimming in slowly heats up.

Teaching others how to treat us must begin with self-respect. If we don't respect ourselves, nobody will. We can teach others how to treat us by setting clear boundaries, speaking our truth and removing ourselves from toxic situations. We can blame the other all we like, but until we decide that enough is enough, life will continue as usual.

Be still and connect with your breath.

Picture the person you need to forgive standing before you. Say to them:

I am willing to forgive you.

I am willing to let go of all toxic emotions I am holding towards you.

I am willing to wish you well.

I am willing to let you go with love.

I am willing to learn and grow from all the lessons of this experience.

Imagine a cord connecting you to the person and the experience, and then cutting that cord. See the person and experience float off into the Light and say:

I let you go with love.

You may need to do this on a regular basis until you feel lighter and freer.

What is forgiveness?

Forgiveness is:

Deciding that **you** don't want to poison yourself by
holding onto blame, anger and resentment
Consciously letting go of toxic emotions and feelings of
revenge
Wishing the other person well
Releasing them and letting them go OR
Taking the knowledge and lessons you've gained from the
event into the future relationship.

Forgiveness is not:

Condoning the other person's behaviour
Dropping boundaries and allowing the other person
into our life at the same level of trust and intimacy that
existed before
Pretending as if the whole thing never happened.

Not forgiving will block your good from coming to you.

Be still and connect with your breath.

As you breathe in, breathe in the healing life force energy and as you breathe out, imagine your heart centre opening.

Feel a sense of spaciousness and light. Say:

Thank You for filling my entire being with Divine Love.

Keep your heart open

♡

To access the vibration of love, ask the Source each morning to fill your entire being with Divine Love.

If you're having difficulties with another person, ask the Source to fill them also with Divine Love.

During difficult interactions, consciously keep your heart open by staying aware of your heartspace. Imagine an invisible cord between your heart and the other person's heart.

You will find yourself being able to **speak from the heart** and the interaction will feel more loving.

Having an open heart not only creates more loving relationships; it creates inner harmony and outer harmony in all areas of your life.

Be still and connect with your breath. Feel into your body. Feel the spaciousness within your body.

The Universe exists within you and you exist within the Universe.

Imagine a cord that connects you to the Heavens and also to the Earth.

Say the following affirmations three times, breathing five times between each:

I am connected to Infinite Intelligence

I allow Infinite Intelligence to run through me

I am Divinely creative

I create Heaven on Earth.

The age of creativity

Our mission at this time in history is to transcend the old paradigm of lack and limitation which we have inherited from our ancestors.

We are now being required to live in a new paradigm of unlimited potential.

The age of productivity has been and gone; the information age has been and gone.

Welcome to the *Age of Creativity* - we are now becoming aware that each of us is a powerful creator and in this world of high-speed change, now more than ever, we need to be present, aware and clear so as to access our innate creativity.

In this moment you have access to the Infinite Intelligence that exists in the Heavens, and you are anchored to the safety and stability of the Earth. You are here to create Heaven on Earth.

Be still and connect with your breath. Ask yourself:

Are there any areas of my life where I am deluding myself with dreams of **happy ever after?**

Consciously breathe out and let go of this old delusion for ten breaths.

Say the following affirmation five times, breathing five times between each:

I now allow my life to be what it is meant to be.

Happy ever after

Many of us were brought up to believe in fairytales - an idealised vision of how we would like our lives to be.

And just like the fairytales we read when we were children, we want our **happy ever after**.

Happy ever after cannot exist on the earth plane. We may manifest our dream, but challenges will keep coming no matter what.

The perfect partner will be a flawed human being like the rest of us, the perfect family will inevitably disappoint us and the dream home will need constant cleaning. That is because we are here to keep growing.

The Buddhists tells us that life is a series of dis-illusionment. With every disappointment, we let go of another illusion.

Every manifestation will have its positive and negative aspect. When we let go of the fairytale, we embrace instead, an authentic and meaningful life.

Be still and connect with your breath.

Contemplate your current struggle.

Ask yourself:

If this were never to change, in what ways would I need to change so as to live with it?

Sit with this question and allow the answers to come forth.

Struggling

Most of us find ourselves struggling with situations at times. Struggling is a part of our journey to become whole.

It is just as much a part as moments of peace and bliss.

We are here to evolve and expand our understanding of love, creativity and who we really are.

We cannot do this without the struggles of life. They are a gift being presented to us for our growth.

If you are experiencing a struggle, surrender to it. Ask yourself **If this were never to change, what qualities would I have to cultivate within myself in order that I feel some semblance of peace?**

Then begin to adopt those qualities. They are what you are meant to be embracing.

Be still and connect with your breath.

Feel yourself present in the here and now.

Know that this present moment is presenting you with opportunities, and that every future present moment will be presenting you with the perfect opportunity if you choose to be present and aware.

Say the following affirmation five times, breathing five times between each:

I embrace each present moment and every opportunity.

Opportunities

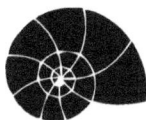

In every moment, opportunities are there for us - an opportunity to make peace with someone, to value ourselves, to learn something new, to do something differently, to heal, to listen, to speak our truth, to help, to give, to receive, to choose again, to walk away, to move towards, to connect, to be still .

Opportunities abound, and yet we miss so many of them because we aren't present and aware enough to see them.

In presence, we greet all opportunities.

Life presents us with one opportunity after another. And if we miss an opportunity, there will be another and another and another.

Be still and connect with your breath.

Say the following affirmation five times, breathing five times between each:

I trust in the process of life and I am safe.

Trust in the process of life

There is a Universal Life Force much greater than ourselves that loves and supports us infinitely - but we will never know this until we begin to trust it.

Our ego mind wants to convince us that we are **all alone in the world** and that we must figure everything out perfectly and **strive** for what we want.

Then we over-plan, second-guess and avoid taking risks. We become anxious.

When we are in the vibration of trusting, life feels easier, and when we begin to trust, we feel more peaceful and at ease and then everything starts falling into place. Sometimes not the place our ego wants, but the place we are meant to be.

When we trust in the process of life, we will be taken care of in the most Divinely right way.

Be still and connect with your breath.

As you watch your breathing, notice how your breath
flows in and out.

Say the following affirmation five times, breathing five
times between each:

I easily let go of the old and allow in the new.

Flow in, flow out

When you become aware, you will realise that all you need will flow to you, and all that you no longer need will exit your life.

This includes jobs, money, people and things.

Life will be a continuous flow of gain and loss and then gain again, and it is all perfect. The ego clings and doesn't like to let go, but we must gracefully let go and cling to nothing.

If we don't, life ceases to flow and we become stuck.

The Universe really does know what is Divinely right for us in any given moment.

Be still and connect with your breath.

Contemplate the things you do that you don't want to do.

Ask yourself:

What is the pay-off I am getting from this?

Sit with this question and allow the answer to emerge.

Pay offs

Most of us do things we don't want to do - eating the wrong foods when we want to be healthy, fighting and blaming when we want peaceful relationships, ignoring or denying opportunities when they appear or procrastinating when we want to move forward.

Why do we do this? The reason isn't always at our level of awareness, but there is always a reason. On the subconscious level, something is **more** important than our conscious goal or desire, such as soothing loneliness, emotional pain or boredom, wanting to be right, wanting to be invisible, wanting to avoid failure, fearing success or wanting to feel safe.

If you're doing something you don't want to do, ask yourself:

What is the pay-off I am getting from of this?

Be still and connect with your breath.

Contemplate any intentions that you have not put into action. Ask yourself:

What is stopping me from taking action?

Allow the answer to emerge.

Say the following affirmation five times, breathing five times between each:

I now release all blocks to acting on my intention.

Good intentions

The road to hell is paved with good intentions ...

Intentions are one thing; acting on them is another.
Intentions mean nothing without aligned action.

The world doesn't respond to your intentions; it responds
to your actions ... the tax office doesn't care that you
meant to pay your taxes, your partner doesn't care that
you **meant** to spend time with him/her but you didn't.

Be still and connect with your breath.

Contemplate if there are any areas of your life where you are being tempted with false promises.

Ask yourself:

What am I refusing to see?

Why?

Say the following affirmation five times, allowing five breaths between each breath.

I choose to see through the eyes of truth.

Too good
to be true

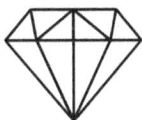

If something seems too good to be true, it probably is. If someone comes into your life and seems too good to be true, they probably are.

Our wounded child longs to be rescued, and she or he will want to believe in wild promises, empty words and quick fixes.

It is tempting to believe what we want to believe, but wise to stand back and ask ourselves if we are being pulled into the path of temptation, which will not lead us to where we think we are going, but in fact in the opposite direction.

If we do choose such a path, rose coloured glasses must come off eventually.

The gift will be in the lesson. It was never going to be in the empty promise.

Be still and connect with your breath.

Contemplate your current challenge. Say the following prayer:

I surrender this challenge to You.

Please do for me what I cannot do, and show me what it is I am meant to learn from this.

Please fill me with your Divine Light and intelligence

So that I may embrace my lesson and transcend this experience.

Thank You.

Lessons

Life is a series of lessons. No challenge is ever presented to us unless there is a valuable lesson to be learned from it.

Until we learn that lesson, the challenge will be presented to us again and again, in various forms, until we learn it.

*If you are going through a challenge right now, reflect upon it and ask yourself **what am I meant to be learning from this?***

You probably will not get an answer immediately, because our conditioning or wounding deems us unable to see. This is why we must call on the Supreme Intelligence to do for us what we cannot do.

Consciously choose to remain open for the lesson or lessons and embrace them when they come.

Once a lesson is fully learned, you won't have to repeat that challenge again, because you have evolved to another level.

Be still and connect with your breath.

Consider now your level of self-confidence on a scale of 1-10 (1 being very low and 10 being very high). Ask yourself:

What is stopping me from feeling more confident within myself?

Say the following affirmation five times, breathing five times between each:

I now embrace the confidence that already exists within me.

Self-Confidence

♡

Self-confidence already exists within you.

It is not something you have to work towards or gain.

If you believe that people and circumstances can rob you of your self-confidence, you disempower yourself.

When you know that nothing and nobody can make you lose your self-confidence without your permission, this shift in perspective will free you and your dreams from being held hostage.

Be still and connect with your breath.

Feel yourself present in this moment.

Say the following affirmations three times, breathing
five times between each:

All I need is in this present moment.

I make plans only where appropriate.

I allow the future to take care of itself.

Plans

"A good plan for today is better than a perfect plan for tomorrow"
- **General Paton**

We all need to make plans, but sometimes we can create unnecessary stress by attempting to plan what cannot yet be planned, attempting to predict things we cannot control, and **second-guessing** the future.

Our ego mind worries constantly about the future and wants to control it, draining us of enjoying the present moment.

And the present moment is all that we have. When we are truly present, we innately know what we can plan and what we cannot.

This frees us to enjoy the present moment, make plans where appropriate and to allow the future to take care of itself.

Be still and connect with your breath.

Feel into your heart space and envision an open and loving space there.

Reflect on where you may be putting up barriers that disconnect you from others.

Ask yourself:

What is it in me that is stopping me from loving this person?

Say the following affirmation five times, breathing five times between each:

I now release all barriers to compassion, and allow my heart to open.

Compassion

Compassion means opening your heart. To live with an open heart requires lowering your emotional barriers and connecting with others with empathy.

Compassion connects you to your own essence and the essence of all those around you.

We cannot keep our hearts open at all times - sometimes we need to protect ourselves - such as being in a situation where we don't feel safe. But taken too far, a lack of compassion can turn to indifference, and indifference can lead to loneliness and isolation.

The key to being more compassionate is realising that we are all one, and that you are in control of your heart and you always have the choice to keep a barrier up or to dissolve that barrier.

Very often the conscious act of compassion can resolve a problem and bring healing to a situation, person or relationship.

Be still and connect with your breath.

Contemplate an area of your life where you feel fearful.

As you breathe in, breathe in the Universe's love, and as you breathe out, consciously send love to the problem or situation.

Say the following prayer:

I surrender this situation to You.

Please bathe this situation in Your Divine love.

Please help me to see this situation through eyes of love

And send me a miracle.

Thank You.

Miracles

Miracles are real, and all miracles must begin with the mind.

When we shift our perspective from fear to love, we create miracles.

If we choose to see our problems lovingly, we create a shift in how we feel.

It is inevitable that this internal shift will create an outer shift - this is the miracle.

If there is an area of your life where you are holding fear, consciously send love to the situation and think of it lovingly.

Prepare yourself for a miracle!

Be still and connect with your breath.

Visualise a tree in the wind. The tree is stable, rooted to the earth and yet its boughs sway with the wind.

Imagine you are that tree, grounded and stable, yet flexible and able to change and move in the moment.

Say the following affirmation five times, breathing five times between each:

I am willing and open to change.

Flexibility

Be willing to change often!

Flexibility means being adaptable to change. It is human nature to be tempted to hold onto What Is.

We've got to learn to bend and flex around every new circumstance, as rigidity robs us of the opportunity to see the freedom of new possibilities.

*We need to be OK with going from **Master** to **Student** again and again and with being in the new and unknown.*

The rate of change is speeding up, and now, more than ever, we must be able to flow with what is coming next, rather than cling to the way things are.

Be still and connect with your breath.

Bring to mind what you are angry about.

As you connect with the feeling of anger, feel the sensations in your body. Ask yourself:

What am I afraid of losing?

What am I afraid could be taken from me?

Acknowledge the fears that come up.

Say the following prayer:

I surrender to You this anger.

Please fill me with Your Light and love

And heal in me all that is creating this anger.

Thank You.

Anger

Our anger is our resistance to the present moment.

The more fearful we are, the more anger we will be holding. It's only when we're afraid that we become angry.

Think of the last time you felt angry, and search for the fear behind it. What were you afraid of losing? What were you afraid would be taken from you?

The more we can get to the root of our anger, and see and address the fear behind it, the more fearless we become - and the less angry we will be.

Think of an angry person - it could be someone you are afraid of.

Can you see how frightened he or she is? If anyone around you is angry, remind yourself that they are frightened, and remove yourself if you are in any danger.

Be mindful of your own anger, and be willing to go beneath it to find its cause.

Be still and connect with your breath.

Feel into your body and all around your body.

Let go of the idea of solidity and see yourself purely as an energy field of awareness. How do you feel?

Say the following affirmation five times, breathing five times between each:

I am an energy field of awareness.

Take this awareness with you in all your interactions.

Field of
awareness

Think of yourself not primarily as a **person** but as a field
of awareness.

When interacting with anyone, give them your fullest
attention. Forget the reason of **why** you are interacting
(buying or selling, wanting information or whatever
it is), and let the field of awareness be your primary
purpose.

This is the most essential factor in any relationship - pure
presence and awareness.

In the field of awareness you open up to much greater
possibilities.

Remarkably, you may find that your original reason for
the interaction will flow more easily, and something even
more precious may come from the interaction.

Be still and connect with your breath.

Reflect on where you may feel resistant to the idea of waiting.

Ask yourself:

Is it in my highest good to wait for this?

If the answer is yes, accept the lesson of waiting.

Say the following affirmation five times, breathing five times between each:

I choose to wait and feel peaceful.

I know that when the time is right, all will be well.

Waiting

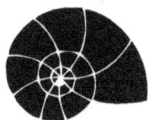

Sometimes the only thing we can do is wait.

At times we must learn to be passive and let nature take its course.

In our modern world of instant gratification, we have forgotten how to wait.

Our greatest treasure is being able to wait for the right moment without becoming bored, anxious, disheartened or indifferent, but instead, having faith that when the time is right, things will move forward.

Be patient, be peaceful.

Be still and connect with your breath. Contemplate what you fear being taken from you.

Remind yourself that if it is truly yours, you have nothing to fear.

And if it is not truly yours, be thankful for the realisation.

Say the following prayer:

I surrender you my fear of losing _____

Please fill me with Your peace

In the knowledge that if _____ is truly mine, there will be no loss,

And that if _____ is not truly mine, it is safe to let go.

Nothing can be taken from you

Nothing that is truly yours can ever be taken from you.

If something is taken from you, know that it was never truly yours to begin with.

Anchor yourself in this knowledge, and you will never fear loss again.

Be still and connect with your breath.

Reflect on where your ego mind gets in the way and feels the need to be **right**.

Imagine now if the desire to be right wasn't there, how differently your interactions could play out.

Say the following affirmation five times, breathing five times between each:

I release the need to be right and allow love to rule.

Let the little things go

Before reacting negatively to someone, ask yourself:

Does this really matter or am I acting out of the need to be right?

The ego loves being right!

In each and every moment we have a choice as to how we respond and that is where our personal power lies.

Do you want to be happy or do you just want to be right?

Be still and connect with your breath. If there is
something you need to know, say the following prayer:

I surrender to You my need to know

_____

I trust that You only ever have my highest good at heart

And that You will show me all that I need to know

In Divine and perfect timing.

Thank You.

Trust that whatever is meant to be revealed to you will
be!

Knowing

Trust that all you need to know will be revealed to you, and that all you do not need to know won't be.

Life really is more simple than what we make it.

Refrain from playing detective and snooping on others - this will not create good karma for you.

Keep to your own business, and if there is anything that is in your highest good to know, be assured that the Universe will show you!

www.ingramcontent.com/pod-product-compliance
Lightning Source LLC
Chambersburg PA
CBHW022004080426
42733CB00007B/470